"Because Katie John is an amusing heroine who acts before thinking and a lovable one who instinctively desires to be friendly, girls will enjoy her adventures."—*Library Journal*

"An excellent story about the everyday adventures of an amiable child. Almost any little girl will recognize herself in Katie John and warm to her immediately."—*Publishers' Weekly*

"The story belongs to Katie John and to the house, and is told with a pace and verve."—*Christian Science Monitor*

"Written with such obvious delight in the subject, such a wealth of convincing details and about such a lovable small girl that it becomes a book to treasure."—Chattanooga *Times*

"A well-written, agreeable story with a likable heroine, lively doings, and a credible ending."—*A.L.A. Booklist*

"A very pleasant and realistic story. All very simple, credible, smoothly written; characterization is consistent and the author has written perceptively of the attitudes of pre-adolescent girls."—*Bulletin of the Center for Children's Books*

KATIE JOHN

KATIE JOHN

by Mary Calhoun

Pictures by Paul Frame

A HARPER TROPHY BOOK
Harper & Row, Publishers
New York, Evanston, San Francisco, London

For my mother and father,
who still live in the old house

KATIE JOHN

First printed in 1960. 11th printing, 1969.

Standard Book Number: 06–440028–x

Contents

KATIE JOHN

The Voice of the Ghost

Morning. Katie John opened her eyes and looked at the strange room. Yes, they were here, all right. She pulled on her blouse and shorts and ran out of the house. Did it really look as horrible as it had when they arrived last night?

Oh, worse. Katie John groaned. It was nothing but an ugly old red brick house, squatting in the sunlight. Square as a box, flat roof, not even a bit of ivy on the walls to soften the sharp corners. It was three stories high, and little hooded windows rimmed the top of the house, like beady eyes. The ugly old box was glaring at her.

"So hah!" Katie John glared back.

Using all her fingers, Katie made a ferocious face at the house. She stretched her eyes and mouth down, shoved her nose up, crossed her eyes, and stuck out her tongue.

"Gaaaah, you old house!"

When Mother had first told her about the house in

3

Missouri, Katie had comforted herself that it might be a beautiful old southern mansion, with huge white pillars on the porch. Well, the house was old, and it had a porch, but the posts were spindly and dirty gray. And it certainly was no mansion. Katie John kicked a post and flopped down on the steps.

Mainly she was mad at the house because it had ruined her whole wonderful summer. If it weren't for the house, she'd be back home in California right now, getting ready to go to the Campfire Girls' camp up in the Sierras. Seemed as if she'd waited all her life to be old enough to go to camp, and now when she was—*whack,* Katie banged the step with her heel—here she was in the backwoods of Missouri. Why, this poky little town wasn't even on a main road.

"I bet they don't even *have* Campfire Girls here," she muttered. "I bet nothing ever *ever* happens here."

It had all come about because Great-Aunt Emily— *poor* Great-Aunt Emily, Katie corrected herself—had died and left the house to Mother. So she and Dad and Mother had driven back East to Barton's Bluff to sell the house.

It might take all summer, Mother said.

Impatiently, Katie ran her fingers up through her thick straight bangs, making her hair stick up in spikes. Then she propped her chin on her hands and stared toward the street. At least this yard wasn't bad. It was big and grassy, and maple trees lined the street beyond the fence.

Katie John studied the fence. It was different from the redwood or neat white picket ones back in California. This was an old-fashioned black iron fence, with iron bars rising to upside-down V's, like a row of jagged teeth. The fence went all across the front of the yard and around the corner, down the side hill. Another iron bar ran under the row of teeth, with enough space in each tooth for a foot.

Katie brightened. Wonder if she could walk that fence?

She ran over to it and swung up, balancing easily. Her head brushed the lower branches of a tree, and down the steep hill she could see the Mississippi River, sparkling blue. Later today she'd go down there, Katie promised herself. But right now, the fence. Katie began to edge sideways, one foot following the other.

"Your Great-Uncle Dick broke his wrist doing that," a voice said calmly.

Katie jerked, caught her balance, and saw a girl standing on the sidewalk. The girl had a round face, with hair smoothly drawn back into pigtails. Her hands were clasped behind her full skirt, and she looked just like a neat, plump little hen. Katie suddenly remembered that she hadn't combed her hair this morning, and she'd worn these shorts for the whole trip.

"How do you know?" Katie demanded. "What happened?"

"I know because your Great-Aunt Emily told me," the girl said. "When he was a little boy he walked the fence and he fell off and broke his wrist. So you'd better get down."

Something about the girl made Katie John feel contrary. The girl seemed so safe and sure, as if she'd never made a mistake or been scolded in her life. Anyway, Katie had made up her mind to walk this fence, and she was going to do it.

"Well, I'm sorry about Uncle Dick," she said, "but he was probably lots younger. I'm not going to fall."

She side-stepped along the fence toward the corner. The plump-hen girl followed.

"I'll catch you when you fall," she said. "I'm Sue Halsey, and I live three doors down the street. I know all about you, too."

Katie stopped. "Who am I?"

"You're Katie John Tucker, and you're ten, same age as me. You live in California, you've come to sell the old Clark house, and I know because—"

"No, I'm not," Katie interrupted. "Katie's in the house. I'm just a runaway orphan. I was hitchhiking along the road and the Tuckers picked me up."

She watched Sue's eyes grow rounder. "Honest?" Sue's smooth face puckered doubtfully.

She looked so uncertain that Katie laughed. Why, she was easy as pie to tease. So easy it wasn't fair to do it.

"No," she grinned. "You're right. I'm Katie John. Come on up." She stretched out a hand to Sue.

"No." Sue started to walk away.

Katie felt a little ashamed. She hadn't meant to hurt the girl's feelings.

"I'll tell you something I'll bet you don't know," she offered.

Sue stopped. "What?"

"When we sell the house we're not going back to California," Katie said, struggling past a bush that threatened to push her off the fence. She turned the corner and started downhill. "We're going to New York City and live on the house money while Daddy finishes the book he's writing."

Privately Katie didn't think much of the idea. In fact, she hated the thought of moving. There wasn't much to do in her home town, but that was where she'd grown up, and that was where all her friends were.

"My!" Sue was sighing. "All right then, I'll tell you something, Katie John Tucker. This old house is haunted!"

"What?" Katie stopped to look at Sue. "Now you're teasing me."

"No, really," Sue insisted. "I heard voices in there."

Sometimes when Miss Clark—Great-Aunt Emily— had been out in the yard, Sue had stopped to talk with her, she explained, but she'd never been in the house. Then one day Miss Clark had asked her to come in because she wanted to give Sue an old doll. Sue had waited in the parlor while Miss Clark had gone to find it.

Sue's voice dropped. "And while she was gone I

heard someone humming and talking softly *right in that room!*"

"Oh, you probably just heard Aunt Emily."

"No, she was way off upstairs," Sue said. "And the voice was right near me. I ran out to the yard and I've never been in that house since."

Voices! Haunted house! Katie John stared at the house. Now that she was around at the side of it, she saw that it wasn't a simple box, after all. It rambled all over the hill at the back, and there were big brick stables behind it.

"Well, you're going in that house now! Show me where it happened," Katie commanded. She started to jump down from the fence, but just then a yelp sounded.

There, racing up the hill, came a small but fierce-looking dog, hauling behind him the tiniest woman Katie had ever seen. The dog was a crazy mixture of Pekingese and fox terrier, with a crinkled Peke face and fluffy tail and a smooth terrier body in between. But the little old woman looked even more odd. Under a large white apron she wore an old-fashioned skirt that brushed the tops of her high-buttoned shoes. Her face was wrinkled and angry, and her nose crooked over like a witch's.

"Ho, Prince, stop, I say!" As she flew along she cried out, "Down from that fence, young lady! Rack and ruin! Oh yes, the poor old Clark place will go to rack and ruin with you wild children in it. Prince, stop!"

The dog only gave a nasty snap at Sue and tore on up the hill, towing the old lady after him.

Katie gawked. "Who was *that?*"

"That's Miss Crackenberry." Sue frowned for the first time. "She hates children. She always thinks we're going to do something awful before we even think of it. And watch out for her precious Prince. He bites."

Katie watched Prince whirl Miss Crackenberry around the corner. "Old Rack and Ruin, hmm?"

Sue giggled. "The perfect name for her. You'll be seeing more of her—and Prince. She lives next door to you, and Prince is always digging up your Aunt Emily's vegetable garden."

Katie jumped down from the fence. "Never mind her now. Show me where you heard the voices."

She ran around to the front door and Sue followed reluctantly. Inside, the hallway was dim after the sunlight. Katie stopped short. "Oh!" A huge animal was looking at her. Then she saw it was only a stuffed moose head on top of a hat and coat rack.

She hadn't seen the inside of the house at all. Last night when they'd arrived she'd been half-asleep, and her dad had tumbled her into a bed. Now she saw that a long stairway with a polished banister rose to the second floor. On the left of the staircase was the room she'd slept in. On the right was a closed door.

Sue opened it. "This is the parlor. It was in here." She stood back. "I'll wait outside."

Katie pulled her arm. "Come on. A voice can't hurt you."

Nevertheless Katie John tiptoed as they entered the deep room. Brown inside shutters were closed at the windows, and in the dark the furniture loomed under shapeless covers. Thick tapestry draperies covered one wall.

"It was over by the piano that I heard it," Sue whispered. "I was sitting on the piano bench."

Katie turned, caught a glimpse of movement across the room, and gasped. A face! Then she let out her breath. It was her own face, reflected in a mirror set back in a tall carved bureau—or something. Anyway it had mirrors and cupboards and shelves cluttered with vases and ornaments.

"Look out!" She poked Sue and pointed toward the bureau.

Sue looked, gasped a little shriek, and crumpled to the floor, hiding her eyes.

"Oh heee!" Katie gurgled with giggles. "Ha-ha-heee!" She collapsed on top of Sue, breathless with laughing. "It's just a mirror!" Still she whispered through her giggles, it was all so shadowy and sort of secret in here.

Sue started to get mad, but Katie whispered, "I'm a ghost!" in such a silly voice that Sue caught the giggles too. They flopped in a heap, squealing with laughter every time they tried to get up.

At last they got untangled and Katie led the way to the piano. "All right now, let's listen." They hushed down and sat on the piano bench. Katie waited for a moment, but she didn't hear anything.

"Maybe it was something in the piano that you heard."

She lifted the folding lid and touched a black key. *Pon-n-n,* the musical note sounded softly in the still room. But when it died away there was no other sound. The girls watched each other with listening eyes.

And then, "I hear something! Shh!" Katie whispered.

There was a little murmur and—yes—a laugh! Now a deeper rumble.

Sue clutched Katie's arm. "I'm leaving!"

"No, you're not! Maybe it's my folks in the hall."

Katie stepped toward the door, but the sound faded immediately. She moved back to the piano bench, and there was the mutter-mutter again. It was a voice, all right! But she couldn't make out the words. Katie slid to the end of the bench, next to the wall, while Sue watched her from the middle of the room. Now the voice was louder. Katie leaned her head against the wall.

And she heard the voice saying, "I'll go see whether Katie's awake."

It wasn't a ghost at all. It was her mother's voice!

"It's my mother!" Katie laughed in relief. "She's talking to Dad."

"But—but that's an outside wall you're listening at." Sue's voice trembled.

Katie looked at the wall, and it was then that she noticed the hole. There in the wallpaper was a small hole, rimmed with china.

"Come here." She motioned to Sue, and put her ear against the hole.

Quite clearly she heard her father say, "Now where's my other shoe?"

"Sue, it's my folks talking in a bedroom somewhere!" Katie cried. "This must be some kind of old telephone system in the walls."

Immediately she stuck her finger into the hole. With her fingertip she felt a little metal passage, and she pushed her whole finger in, trying to feel farther.

"I'll call my folks through here," Katie giggled. "Won't I give them a surprise!"

But when she tried to pull her finger out, she couldn't. It was stuck in the small opening.

"Sue, I'm stuck. Help pull."

"A speaking tube! So that's all the ghost voice was," Sue chattered. "Here, try to twist your finger—I should have known. Mom says old Miss Clark had all kinds of funny gadgets built into this house. . . . Can't you pull?"

But Katie's finger was stuck tight and swelling.

"Hurry, go get my mother," Katie half-giggled, half-sobbed, "before I grow fast to this crazy old house."

Sue ran to the hall and shouted up the stairs, while Katie tried to call into the speaking tube. Her finger had plugged the hole too neatly, however, for her voice to get through.

Katie's mother ran down the stairs in her bathrobe, crying, "What—what—who?" at the sight of a strange girl in the hall. "What's the matter?" Katie's dad called, clattering down behind her. They hurried into the parlor, where they saw their daughter hooked to the wall by one finger.

"Katie John Tucker!" exclaimed her mother. "Are you in trouble before I can even get up in the morning?"

"Mother, I'm sorry, it was—" "Ghost . . . voices," Katie and Sue talked at once. "Speaking tube in the wall and then—"

Katie's mother threw up her hands. "Never mind! Stop! Let me get you loose and then you can tell me."

She hurried away and brought back soap and a wet washrag. While she soaped Katie's finger, Katie's dad grinned down at her.

"Stop wiggling," he told her mildly. "The old house likes you. It was just trying to get a good hold on you."

Katie laughed as her sore finger slipped out of the hole, but she set her chin. "Well, it hasn't got me yet!"

Katie Helps Out

Katie John was sweeping down the front stairs. And what a long, dull job it was. Eighteen steps from the third floor to the second, and twenty steps down to the first floor. Then she had to dust the parlor. She and Sue had big plans for this morning. They were going to make a tree house. But at this rate she'd never get down to Sue's.

"I hate and despise housework!" Katie muttered, whisking a pile of dust down to the next step. "When I grow up I'm going to be rich and have somebody else do all the work."

She wondered if maybe she was allergic to dust. She wiggled her nose, but it didn't feel sneezy.

Housework wouldn't be so bad if there were some fun to it. Like the other day, when she was sweeping down the back stairs. Halfway down her broom had caught on the edge of the step, and the step had opened up, just like the lid of a box. All the steps opened from there on down, and she'd found all sorts of things.

15

Great-Aunt Emily must have been a very neat, saving woman. There were folded paper bags, balls of string, jars of nails, and in one step box upon box of buttons—sparkly, colored, and beaded ones. Looking at them, Katie had forgotten all about sweeping until Mother had come along.

Now Katie had her pile of dust almost to the bottom of the stairs when she heard voices in the parlor. She peeked through the crack of the parlor door and saw Mother talking to that old Miss Crackenberry.

The tiny old lady was perched on the love seat with her ankles crossed just so. Prince was there, too, gnawing on the leg of the center table. "That dear little cherrywood table!" Mother had cried when she saw it the first day. Now Mother kept giving Prince worried looks as the nasty little dog chewed away, but of course she was too polite to say anything. And Miss Crackenberry didn't seem to notice. She was too busy talking.

"What an odd name for a girl—Katie *John,*" Katie heard her say. "Why ever did you give her a man's name?"

None of your business, Katie thought. She hated for people to talk about her when she wasn't around. That is, when they didn't know she was around.

Katie knew all about her name. Mother had always wanted to name her child after her own father. And when she, Katie, was born, Mother said she might never have a boy, so she named her Katie John, just to make sure.

Lucky thing, too, because no brothers or sisters had come along yet.

But all that was private. Thank goodness, Mother must think so, too, because she only said, "It's an old family name."

Katie hurried back to the stairs, to finish up quickly. Sue would be waiting; Sue wouldn't know how to start on the tree house. Hurry, hurry—Katie swept the dust into a dustpan, emptied it back in the kitchen trash sack, and got the dustrag.

She walked into the parlor, and Mother introduced her to Miss Crackenberry, who gave her a disapproving nod. Katie attacked the bookcase with the dustrag.

"Wait until later, Katie," Mother reproved. "We have company now."

"Then can I go down to Sue's?" Katie said instantly.

"No, I want you to finish before you play. Sit down with us."

"But the morning will be gone!" Katie cried, pushing her bangs into spikes. With a swish of the cloth, she finished off the bookshelves.

"Katie—"

"Really, I can be done in just a minute—" She swiped at the fireplace mantel.

"Katie!"

"But, *Mother*—"

Miss Crackenberry's lips stretched into a thin smile. "Headstrong," she said in a satisfied voice.

Katie saw her mother blush. She stopped dusting and sat down with the dirty dustrag in her lap.

"I'm sorry—I—" She shut her mouth. Maybe she'd better just keep quiet.

Miss Crackenberry started talking about how she'd miss Aunt Emily, but she kept looking at the clock on the mantelpiece.

Maybe she'll leave soon, Katie thought. And look what that Prince was doing to the table leg! Scratches all over! Katie snapped her fingers at the dog, but he only turned his eyes and growled through his chewing. Couldn't Miss Crackenberry hear the table rattling under his teeth?

No, Miss Crackenberry was going on and on about Aunt Emily and how they'd miss her work at the Altar Guild at church. Katie watched her crook-nose bob as she talked. Even across the room she could smell the old lady, a dry, sickish-sweet smell, like old medicine. She wondered if Aunt Emily really had been a good friend of Miss Crackenberry's. She hoped not, because anybody that was a friend of this witch-lady—well! Probably not, for Mother certainly had loved Aunt Emily.

At last Miss Crackenberry was getting ready to leave.

"Oh yes," she added, "Emily always meant to give me something to remember her by, but she didn't have a chance before she passed on. Suppose I just take some little thing you wouldn't want anyway."

She peered around the room and then seemed to see

the clock for the first time. "How about that ugly old clock?"

It was a tall clock, made of white marble, and as if in reply it struck the half-hour with a cracked bong.

"Oh dear," Mother said hastily, "I'm afraid that clock shouldn't go out of the family."

Katie had heard the story of the clock. Aunt Emily's father used to collect things like that and paint pictures of them. He bought the clock at an auction, but it was too heavy to carry. So he bought a wheelbarrow, too, and wheeled the clock home in it.

At Mother's words, Miss Crackenberry pursed her mouth until her nose almost touched it.

Mother added, "I'll give you one of Aunt Emily's rings. I'm sure that would be much nicer."

Prince and Miss Crackenberry left right after Mother brought the ring.

Katie burst out indignantly, "She just came to get that clock! She kept looking at it all the time."

"I know, honey," Mother chuckled. "Aunt Emily once told me that old clock is a collector's item, worth two hundred dollars. I expect Miss Crackenberry knew it, too. . . . Never mind, she's just a lonely old lady."

"Talk about headstrong," Katie muttered. "*She* is!"

Then she looked at Mother uneasily.

"Am I—am I headstrong?"

Mother smiled down at her. "Well, you are pretty set on your own way," she said gently. "But you aren't mean about it. It's just that you plunge so eagerly at things that you don't stop to think, honey."

Katie's face drooped. "I guess—"

Mother smoothed her cheek. "Don't worry. You've got a sunny heart, and that's what matters. You'll stop to think more as you grow up."

Still Katie hesitated. She'd embarrassed Mother in front of Miss Crackenberry. If she was so good-hearted . . . Slowly she brought the words out.

"I guess—I don't have to go to Sue's this morning. I guess—I'd better help you."

Mother gave her a proud smile. "Well, I was going to hunt eggs this morning. You could do that for me."

Great-Aunt Emily had kept chickens in a runway between the back yard and the vegetable garden. Mother and Dad had been too busy to do anything but feed the chickens, so no one had gathered eggs since Aunt Emily died. Katie was to find all the eggs she could and put them in a big box.

"We'll leave them in the alley for the garbage man," Mother said. "They're probably all rotten."

"Rotten!"

"Pretend you're hunting Easter eggs." Mother laughed. "But be careful not to break them!"

Hunting rotten eggs! That was a fine job for a bright Monday morning. But she couldn't back out now. After she dusted the parlor, Katie found a cardboard box in the basement and went out to the chicken yard.

This was the worst-looking part of the whole place. All the chicken-wire fencing was rickety and leaned crazily, and trash was scattered around a couple of dirty wooden sheds. It looked like a junk yard. Dad was there, trying to prop up part of the fence with a post.

"Katie girl!" Dad greeted her. "Want to help?"

"All right, only I have to hunt rotten eggs first—ugh."

"Go ahead then." Her father laughed at her disgusted face. "I'm only fixing it temporarily anyway. This whole chicken run is an eyesore. We'll gradually kill off the chickens and eat them while we're here. Then I'll tear down all this ragged fencing."

Katie set her box down, shooed the chickens away from her feet, and started to hunt for eggs. "Has anyone come to buy the house yet?" she called to Dad.

"Not yet." He hammered the post into the ground. "Big old houses are dime-a-dozen in this town."

In between writing on his book, Dad was doing repair jobs on the place so it would have a better chance to sell. Just the same, he was always coming up from the cellar or down off the roof, saying, "House is solid, though. Ninety years old, and not a crack in the foundation. They don't build 'em like this any more."

Now Katie scrabbled through the weeds and found two eggs. Nose wrinkled, she carried them over to the box and gingerly laid them in the bottom. All around her the fat white chickens scratched and clucked busily. Over in the fence corner was another nest of eggs, four this time.

Back and forth Katie went, piling eggs in the carton. Some were cracked and gummy-looking. She was careful not to get them near her nose.

Presently she saw a hen with ragged feathers squat under a bush by the gate. In a moment the hen rose and squawked happily. There was a new egg that hadn't been there before.

Well, I *know* that one is fresh, Katie thought. I'll take it in to Mother.

She picked up the egg and pushed open the gate. It was as ramshackle as the fence, however, and it buckled when she tried to shut it. While she struggled, the ragged-feathered hen darted through the opening and ran clucking into the back yard.

"Come back here!" Katie called. "Oh, fiddle. Dad!"

But Dad had gone to the basement for something. Still holding the new egg, Katie ran after the hen. "Shoo!" She motioned it back toward the gate. "Squawk!" went the hen, and it skittered wildly around the yard, trying to flap its wings. Katie darted after it. "Get in there!"

Back and forth, around the yard, Katie panted after the hen. Now she had it cornered in a bush. No, the hen turned and skipped past her. Katie whirled, tripped, and fell smash on the new egg. She lay there for a second, feeling the mess soak into her blouse.

"You—you chicken!" she screamed. She scrambled up, dripping goo, and ran to the box of rotten eggs. "Let's see how *you* like egg all over you!"

She snatched up an egg and threw it at the hen. The hen dodged. And the egg smattered on the back walk. A horrible smell rose in the air.

"All right for you!" Katie yelled, and threw another egg. Missed again. The old hen dodged and squawked frantically as Katie threw egg after egg. Smash, splatter—*phew*, the stink! Then she hit the hen square on the side. It let out a startled yelp and hopped straight up in the air.

"Got you!" Katie shrieked, reaching for another egg.

"Katie! Stop!" Dad came running out of the basement. "*Katie John Tucker!* What under the sun do you think you're doing!"

Katie stopped. Slowly she laid the rotten egg back in

the box. The fever of battle faded and the overpowering stench came at her full force. The whole yard shimmered with it. It was stifling.

"I guess I didn'd thing," she whimpered, holding her nose.

Dad waved his arms in the air. "Rotten eggs all over the place! That poor old hen! Katie, how could you!"

Katie sobbed, which wasn't easy, holding her nose.

Dad looked down at her, and the corner of his mouth quirked. He set it firmly, saying, "All right, go change your blouse. Then come back here and help me clean up this mess."

Katie stopped snuffling and ran for the house. Maybe she'd never learn to think first. But one thing she knew for certain. When Dad killed the chickens she wasn't going to eat any. Chickens were too ornery.

Katie John, Detective

Katie John walked bent over, searched the sidewalk. There. There was another one. A spot of blood! She'd seen the trail of blood specks coming out of a garage and was following it.

"Katie, what are you doing?" Sue came out of her house.

"Detective work," Katie said mysteriously. She straightened up to rub her back and wipe the sweat off her face. It was already hot this morning.

"See?" she said. "Blood. A trail of blood! It came out of that garage down the street. Maybe somebody carried a dead body to the river and dumped it in."

"Oh, Katie!" Sue said. "Probably somebody just cut himself."

"No," Katie insisted. "If you cut yourself, would you walk along dripping blood? You'd wrap up the cut. Come on, let's see where it goes."

The trail led past Katie's house, across the street, and

25

along the bluff above the river. Once they lost the trail, but farther along they found another dried red spot. Then the spots stopped. Katie went ahead for half a block, but she couldn't find any more.

"Maybe whoever it was just stopped bleeding," Sue suggested. "Let's go back to your house."

"You're no detective," Katie said scornfully. "If the trail stops here on the sidewalk, then it must go over the bluff down to the river. We'll search the grass."

The steep hillside was a tangle of bushes, weeds, and trees, a small jungle between the town and the river's edge. Katie got down on her knees and hunted carefully through the grass.

"Sue!" she called. "Here's a spot on a grass blade. Come on, poky!"

Sue stayed on the sidewalk. "Look." She pointed.

Down there under a bush was a cat. She was eating something. It might have been a mouse, though there wasn't much left to tell.

"Oh, Katie!" Sue giggled. "Detective Katie, hunting down a mysterious dead mouse!"

Katie John watched the cat in disappointment. She shrugged. "Oh well, it *might* have been a dead body. People ought to keep track of things like that. The police can't be everywhere, you know."

Faint shouts came from below, and Katie saw some children running through the trees farther down the hill. They had blankets rigged into a kind of tent. A worn path wound down the bluff.

"Sue, let's go down and play."

Sue shook her head. "They're wild rough kids from the river shacks. My mother won't let me play in the jungle."

"Oh, all right," Katie said, scrambling after her. "Let's go home. It's getting too hot to be outdoors anyway."

Katie's house was cool and shadowy after the morning sun. The walls were thick, and Katie's mother had closed the inside shutters to keep out the sun. Sue wanted to play dolls, but Katie didn't care much for dolls. She saw Great-Aunt Emily's old cat, Lulu, curled up in a chair in the parlor.

"Instead of dolls, let's dress up Lulu in your doll

clothes," Katie suggested. "We could take her for a ride in your doll buggy."

Lulu laid her ears back as Katie picked her up.

"She looks sort of grouchy," Sue said doubtfully. "But we can try."

Lulu was struggling now, so the girls decided not to carry her down to Sue's house. Instead they'd go get the doll clothes and bring them back here. Just so Lulu wouldn't get away, Katie put the cat in her room and shut the door.

"Mother," she called to the back of the house, "don't open the door to my room. I've got the cat shut in there."

"All right," Mother answered.

The girls ran down the street to Sue's house. Sue shared a room with her big sister, Janet, and her side of the room had dolls all around. She even had a tiny dresser full of doll clothes. Sue picked out the biggest doll dresses, as Lulu was quite a fat, fluffy old cat.

When they went back to Katie's house and opened her bedroom door, there was no sign of Lulu.

Mother said she hadn't opened the door, and Dad had been upstairs trying to write all morning.

Katie and Sue hunted under all the furniture, but no cat. At last Katie stood in the middle of her room and sighed in exasperation.

"Well, how could she get out? . . . Wait—maybe —Sue! I know! This room has a secret door. A secret passage, maybe! That's how she got out!"

"But—but how could a cat open a secret door?"

"I don't know," Katie said impatiently, "but she's lived here longer than we have. She'd learn how."

It was the perfect answer. Great-Aunt Emily was always building strange things into the house—the phone system in the walls, those steps with the lids. Why not a secret door? Here was a real mystery to solve!

Mother laughed, "Have fun, girls," and went back to her vacuuming.

In the books, Katie said, there was always a wall panel that sounded hollow or a little button to push. And they'd better look down low where Lulu could reach the button. The girls circled the room on their knees, tapping the wall and watching for strange little buttons or holes. But no little doors flew open, no walls slid silently aside.

Almost every room in the house had a fireplace, and Katie's room had one, too. Now Sue noticed that the fire screen was ajar.

"Oh, fiddle," Katie said, taking the screen away. "Here, kitty."

But Lulu wasn't there, either. Then the girls noticed that there was something different about this fireplace. The chimney not only went up, but the opening at the back also went down in a tunnel toward the cellar.

Katie stuck her head into the fireplace and called, "Kitty kitty kitty?" Sure enough, a faint "meow" came from below.

"She's in the cellar!" Katie jumped up. "Come on."

She and Sue pounded down the basement stairs. The basement was a maze of rooms under the house. There were storerooms, a laundry room, coal cellar, furnace room, and even a small apartment where servants had lived in the old days. Katie paused to figure out which part would be under her room, and led the way through the coal cellar to a wooden door fitted into the brick wall.

Yes, Lulu's yowls were coming from beyond the door. Katie tugged at the door until she got it open. Immediately the cat ran out, fur on end, and dashed for the basement stairs.

Katie started after her, but Sue warned, "Let her go. She's too mad to play with now. She'd scratch."

"All right." Katie came back. "I want to see this room anyway."

The little room was almost cold, and dark, with just one dirty windowpane set high in the wall at ground level. Katie John stepped inside and wrinkled her nose. What a strange, musty smell. The walls and floor were damp, and the room smelled of earth and age. It was an old, old smell, shut up for how long? Katie sniff-sniff-sniffed. She liked it, the same way she liked the smell of exhaust gas from cars.

"Smell, Sue," she said happily. "Isn't it wonderful? I'm going to come down here and sniff every once in a while."

But where had Lulu come out? Katie found the place, a sort of metal chute coming out of the wall.

"I bet that old cat was surprised when she came sliding down there," Katie giggled.

Sue laughed too, but hugged her elbows. "Let's go now. It's cold in here."

"All right, but let's explore the rest of the cellar while we're down here. We still might find a secret passage," Katie said without much hope.

The more she thought about it, though, the more certain she was. After all, this was a very old house. Great-Grandfather Clark had had it built right after the Civil War. People always put in secret rooms in those days, didn't they? And the walls were so thick there could be a walled-in place somewhere—surely! Katie began to hunt with new eagerness.

"Let's start with that little servants' apartment," she said. "I've never been in there."

The apartment had three rooms: a large kitchen where all the cooking was done for the house in the old days, a tiny sitting room, and a bedroom. Also a long bathroom, complete with tub.

"This house has more bathrooms," Katie said. "That's the sixth one I've found."

"I know," Sue nodded. "My mother says your Great-Aunt Emily had very modern ideas about being clean. She had all those extra bathrooms put in fifty years ago."

The girls had been knock-knocking on all the walls.

"Oh, Katie, there's nothing down here," Sue urged. "Someplace upstairs would be a better place to hunt."

"Wait." Katie had her head in a big cupboard by the kitchen table. "Now that's funny."

Sue put her head in too. There were no shelves inside, only a large empty space. The girls looked up, and the emptiness went as far as they could see.

"Now, what . . . ?" Katie puzzled. "It isn't big enough for a room. . . . What are these ropes?"

Two heavy cords stretched up along one wall of the cupboard. Katie pulled on a cord. And the bottom of the cupboard moved. "Sue!" she cried, and pulled harder. The bottom stuck for a moment and then, with a scraping sound, rose like a platform, up through the cupboard.

"Keep pulling!" Sue jumped up and down. "See what's underneath."

Katie pulled until the platform was above their heads, then peered down in the cupboard. She saw nothing but thick cobwebs and a bare floor.

"What *is* this thing? I'm going to keep pulling the cord until something happens."

She did. But all that happened was that the platform finally stopped somewhere up in the darkness. Katie pulled the other cord, and the platform started down again.

"Let's see where it comes out upstairs!" Katie cried.

She ran for the cellar stairs, with Sue after her. On the first floor the girls stopped to get their bearings.

"Now it was in this wall," Katie figured. "It must come up in the dining room."

Yes, there on the right wall was another set of cupboard doors, just like those in the basement kitchen.

Katie pulled open the doors, and there was the platform. She looked up, but the opening stopped just above her head.

"Here's where the platform comes, but why?"

"Maybe it's some kind of little elevator for the servants," Sue suggested.

"Oh, silly," Katie laughed. "Can't you see a fat cook on that little platform? Only a child could ride on that." She stopped. "Say!"

"No, Katie!" Sue cried.

"Yes!" Katie was already folding her legs up onto the platform. "Now you just pull the rope slow and easy."

"It might break," Sue worried. "You'd be killed!"

"It's as strong as new." Katie bounced on the platform. "See?"

"All right," Sue said unhappily.

She pulled on the rope, and the platform, with Katie curled up on it, began to descend. The board scraped and squeaked against the sides of the cupboard as Katie's head disappeared below.

"Are you all right?" Sue called down.

"Fine. The walls are all cobwebby, but it's fun!" Katie's voice sounded hollow, as if she were down a well. "Just like Alice in Wonderland going down the rabbit hole. Wait 'til you try it."

It was dark and hot here between the walls, but Katie John shivered with excitement. This was the most . . . the most *mysterious* adventure she'd ever had. Nothing back home had ever been like this. But then, she'd never lived in a house like this before.

She was beginning to like this old house. There was always something new to find out about it. Like peeling an onion, with always a fresh layer underneath.

The platform jerked and stopped.

"What's the matter?" Katie called up to where a faint gray light showed at the opening.

"The rope's stuck!" Sue answered.

"Maybe it's catching on the pulley."

"No." Sue tugged at the cords. "It just won't move!"

"Oh, Sue," Katie's voice echoed up the hole. "You just don't try. I'll have to climb out."

Sue leaned into the cupboard. But the platform had gone more than halfway down, and, even when Katie stood up, they couldn't reach each other.

"What shall we do?" Sue whimpered.

Katie felt around in the dark for something to climb on, but the walls were smooth.

"Guess I'll just have to stay here." She tried to laugh.

"Oh-h-h," Sue wailed.

Katie sighed. There was no getting around it. "Go get my mother," she told Sue.

While Sue was gone. Katie carefully sat down on the platform. She hoped the rope wouldn't let go suddenly and send her crashing to the basement. It was so dark she could barely see, and cobwebs kept waving out and brushing her face. It must be like this inside a tomb, all shut up. Except that in a tomb there was no air. Katie wished she hadn't thought of that. She took a deep breath, and another. Her heart began to pound. Of course there was plenty of air in here, she told herself sternly. There was the opening right up there. . . . Oh, thank goodness! There was Mother's face peering down.

"Katie John Tucker! Are you down there?"

"Yes, Mother." Katie's voice trembled.

"But how did you—what—just wait 'til I get you out of there, young lady!"

Katie only hoped she could.

First Mother tried to pull the cord, but it wouldn't budge.

"Maybe Dad will have to chop through the wall," Katie called faintly.

"We'll try from below. Come with me, Sue."

Their faces disappeared, and Katie was alone again. For a long, long time she sat cramped on the board, with the walls rising close around her. At last she felt the board jerk under her. Katie clutched at it, but it didn't fall. Slowly the platform sank, scraping against the walls. And here she was in the basement kitchen again.

"Oh, Mother!" Katie tumbled out of the cupboard and hugged her mother. "We were just exploring a mystery."

"Katie, Katie, you and your mysteries!" Mother squeezed her tightly. "It's just an old dumb-waiter."

"Long ago it was used to hoist food to the dining room,"

she explained. "The cook put the food on the shelf and sent it up, saving herself trips up and down stairs carrying all the food for Great-Grandpa's big family."

"Oh," said Katie. "Well, just the same, it was one of the best adventures I ever had!"

It was, too, now that the scare was over and she was all right. She hesitated.

"Are you going to punish me?"

Mother looked at her for a long moment. "I remember I wanted to ride in the dumb-waiter when I was a little girl," she said thoughtfully, "but Grandpa wouldn't let me. . . . No-o," she decided. "Sometimes a good adventure is worth a little trouble. . . . But don't you ever try this one again, young lady!"

Katie hugged her mother happily as she promised. What a good thing mothers were young once!

There's Nothing Like a Good Idea

Katie and Sue had money trouble. Fifty cents' worth of movie-ticket-money trouble, to be exact. *Little Women* was coming to the Grand Theater tomorrow afternoon, and the girls had been reading the book all week in preparation—Katie had declared for Jo, and Sue loved pretty Amy. However, Katie John's allowance was long gone, and Sue had only a dime.

"I should think you'd want me to see it," Katie had argued with her father. "It's a children's classic."

But Dad had said that the book was the classic, not the movie, and she was welcome to read the book. The fact that she already had didn't sway him. Katie was supposed to get along on her allowance.

"It isn't fair," she wailed to Sue, as they sat on Katie's front steps. "This movie is so old it'll never come around again."

She faced the thought of not seeing Jo alive in color and gave a little groan.

37

Sue curled the end of her pigtail around her finger as she thought. "Maybe we could earn the money," she suggested.

Well now, there was a thought. The girls discussed the possibilities of pulling weeds or running errands.

Then, "I know!" Katie cried. "We could have a lemonade stand! And it would be fun, too, not like pulling weeds out in the hot sun."

"I don't know," Sue said doubtfully. "I had a lemonade stand once, and hardly anybody bought any."

"If there was something special about it, they would. Something extra. . . ." Katie thought about it. "Hey, what about popcorn? Free popcorn!" The idea gathered fire. "And the popcorn would make them thirsty for lemonade!"

"Oh, Katie!" Sue hugged her. "That's a wonderful idea!"

It was a pretty tremendous idea, at that, Katie thought, very satisfied with herself. Strange that the people didn't do it at all those orange-juice stands along the highways back in California. Maybe if she ever got back there, she could sell them the idea!

Now, though, the first thing was to make the stand. The girls found some wooden boxes in the brick barn behind the house. They lugged them around to the front and set them up on the grass between the sidewalk and the street. Katie got Sue a paintbox and some paper, and Sue set to work painting signs—LEMONADE, 5¢ A GLASS and FREE POPCORN. Even if they sold only ten glasses of lemonade, the girls figured, they'd have enough money for the movie, and then they could use Sue's dime for candy.

Katie went into the house to make popcorn. In the kitchen Mother was up to her elbows in canning peaches. Kettles boiled on the stove, finished jars of peaches stood on the counter, a bushel basket of peaches sat on the floor, and the room was hot with sweet-smelling steam.

When Katie told her about the lemonade stand idea, Mother said, "I'll tell you a surer way to earn some money. I'll pay you and Sue fifty cents if you'll pit all the peaches in that basket."

Katie looked at the almost-full basket. Selling lemonade would be a lot more fun than pitting peaches in this hot kitchen.

"Do you really need us? I mean, we've already got the stand set up and—"

Mother laughed. "Oh, never mind. Go ahead with your lemonade project."

Katie set to work in a whirl. She could hardly wait to see how much money they'd earn. She put some oil and popcorn kernels in a skillet and began shaking it over the fire. Sue came in from painting signs, and Mother cleared a corner of the kitchen counter for her to squeeze lemons.

Now the kernels were popping and pinging away against the skillet lid. Katie jiggled the pan vigorously and wiped her damp face. If they sold lots of lemonade today, they could do it tomorrow—every day—why, they'd be rich!

At last the skillet felt full and the popping had stopped. Katie lifted the lid and peeked in. Pop! Pop! Two puffs of popcorn flew out. She set the pan back on the stove, rescued one of the kernels from the floor and ate it. The other kernel had landed in an open jar of peaches, and she fished it out. Umm! It tasted good—sweet and peach-flavored.

Say, maybe she'd discovered something new. Peach-flavored popcorn! Should they try dipping all the popcorn in peach juice?

"Katie! The popcorn!" Sue cried, rushing to the stove, where Katie had left the skillet sitting on the flame.

However, when they poured the popcorn into a big bowl, they found that only the bottom layer was a little burned. Katie and Sue ate most of the burned pieces and the old maids.

"After all," Katie said, "it's free. People shouldn't mind a few burned pieces. We'll put lots of butter on it."

Maybe they'd better forget about peach-flavored popcorn until some other time. Sue had the lemonade all ready now. But even with plenty of water and ice cubes, there wasn't very much, for Mother had had only a few lemons on hand.

"There aren't ten glasses there," Sue decided. "Here, Katie."

She took her handkerchief from her pocket and untied the dime in the corner. They'd just have to use the dime to buy more lemons. While Katie ran over to the little grocery store, Sue would sell what lemonade they had.

Katie helped Sue carry the popcorn and lemonade out to the stand and ran down the street to the store. Flower's Grocery was only two blocks away, but her face burned like fire by the time she got there. Well, it was a good thing the morning was so hot—more people would be thirsty for lemonade.

Mr. Flower was puffing as he reached down a can of beans from a high shelf for an old lady. Katie thought Flower was such a funny name for him. The storekeeper was fat, with a round red face, and he looked more like a beet than a flower. He was nice, though.

Mr. Flower put the old lady's groceries in a sack and turned to Katie with a big smile. "Hot enough for you?"

Katie grinned. "I'm glad it's hot. Makes people thirsty." She told him all about the lemonade stand and the free popcorn.

Well now, Mr. Flower thought that was just grand. A right smart idea. He was always glad to see youngsters go into business. Let's see, just for Katie, he'd make a special price on the lemons. He'd give her four.

"Oh, thanks!" Katie took the sack. "Come by our stand and we'll give you some lemonade free."

She ran home. So far all she'd done was work. Now for the fun part, selling lemonade and collecting money.

But when she reached the stand, the money box was still empty, the popcorn bowl was almost empty, and Sue was in tears.

"Some big boys came by," Sue sobbed, "and they ate the popcorn all up!"

She'd tried to stop them, but the boys had pointed out that the sign said "free popcorn." And they didn't want any lemonade because they were on their way downtown to buy root beer.

"Ver-ry funny." Katie scowled. "We'll just have to make more popcorn and change the sign to 'One hand-ful of popcorn free.' Come on, Sue, don't cry."

Grimly the girls set to work again. By now, getting ready wasn't fun at all. Here the morning was half-gone, and they hadn't sold one glass of lemonade yet. This time Sue made the popcorn to be sure it didn't burn, and Katie made more lemonade in the big pitcher.

"Where's the sugar, Mother?"

"In the can next to the flour." Mother was almost done with the peaches.

Katie measured the sugar into the pitcher. What else? If she put in a little red food coloring, it would look like pink lemonade. She shook a few drops into the pitcher. Now to mix it up. Katie got the egg beater and beat hard. Oh, what a gorgeous pink froth! How could anyone resist buying such lovely lemonade!

"Now!" said Katie.

And the girls carried their wares out to the stand. They settled to wait for customers. After all that work, their throats were so hot and dry. . . . They stared at the beautiful pitcher of icy pink lemonade. But no, they mustn't drink any. They had to sell all of it to earn enough movie money.

"We must be strong," Katie said, looking away from the pink froth. "Don't look at the popcorn, either. It'll only make us thirsty."

It was hard not to smell the popcorn, though.

Here came someone. Oh, it was only Miss Crackenberry, with Prince tugging ahead at his leash. She was probably too stingy to buy lemonade. Anyway, Katie didn't think she wanted Miss Crackenberry for her first customer. The girls watched to see what the little old woman would do.

Prince ran sniffing straight to the popcorn bowl. Katie put her hands protectively around it. Now Miss Crackenberry was slowing, opening her thin mouth. . . .

"Have you girls got a business license?" she snapped. And trotted on.

Katie gasped and laughed in spite of herself. Trust Old Rack and Ruin to say something mean.

"Should we have a license?" Sue worried.

"No!" Katie snorted. "She's just being her usual mean self."

Again they settled to wait. Now a small man with a big white mustache came hurrying along the sidewalk. It was Mr. Follensbee, the real estate man who was trying to sell the house. He lived in an apartment house on the next corner.

"Well, well, girls," he said, pausing at the stand. "Lemonade, eh? Just the thing for a hot day, eh? All right, here's a nickel."

"Oh, thank you!" Katie put the nickel in the money box while Sue poured out a glassful of lemonade.

Mr. Follensbee took a big swallow. "Ahh—gh!" The pink froth stood on his white mustache. He looked into the glass and then at the girls. They smiled back.

"*Pink* lemonade?" he asked nervously.

"Yes, isn't it delicious?" Katie said.

"Um—oh yes." He took another little sip and his mustache quivered. Mr. Follensbee set down the glass and wiped his mouth. "Yes, yes," he said, and he hurried away as if he was afraid they'd stop him.

"Now, wasn't he funny?" Sue said, looking at the still half-full glass. "He acted as if he didn't like it."

"Oh well." Katie poured the remains of the glass on the ground. "Maybe he didn't like getting lemonade all over his mustache."

"Oh dear," Sue said. "Here comes Janet. I suppose she's going to make fun."

Katie saw Sue's big sister, Janet, walking along with her friend, Carolyn. The girls wore white shorts and carried tennis rackets, so they must be on their way to the park. Janet was all curvy and tan, and she was really quite pretty. Too bad she wasn't as nice as she looked. She always treated Sue and Katie John as if they were *little* girls, and acted as if she knew just about everything in the whole wide world.

"Oh, my goodness," Janet laughed. "Look here, Caro —a lemonade stand! Remember how we used to try to sell lemonade when we were little?"

Katie and Sue squirmed and looked crossly at nothing. But Janet had stopped at the stand.

"The lemonade looks good," she said kindly now. "Let's have some, huh, Caro?"

She gave Sue a dime, and Katie brightened as she poured out two glassfuls.

"Umm." Janet took a sip. And then stopped, clutching her throat. "Ack!" She spit out the drink. "What *is* this stuff?"

Carolyn was gagging too. "What did you put *in* it?"

"Why, it's just lemonade with red food coloring," Sue said, bewildered. "What's the matter with it?"

"It tastes horrible, that's all!" Janet said, her lips stretched down in disgust. "It tastes like soap!"

"Let's see." Katie took a sip. "P-tooey! Oh-h. You're right."

"It was all right when I made it," Sue said, "because I tasted it. You must have done it when you made the second batch, Katie."

"Oh no," Katie moaned. "All this lemonade gone to waste. But what happened?"

"Maybe you stuck your finger in it," Janet giggled, and the big girls laughed as if that was terribly funny.

They demanded their dime back and went on to the park, while Katie and Sue fled to the house to see what could have happened. Katie examined the little red food coloring bottle and even let a drop fall on her tongue. No soap taste there. Mother had the kitchen cleaned up from the peach canning, and was getting lunch ready now. She was very sorry about the lemonade fiasco, but she couldn't imagine what had gone wrong, either.

"I squeezed the lemons," Katie checked step by step, "and added water right from the faucet, and got the sugar from here."

"Oh, heavens!" shrieked Mother. "That isn't sugar, that's my granulated laundry soap!"

"No!" Katie gasped. "No wonder the lemonade frothed up so pretty when I beat it!"

"No wonder!" Sue echoed in dismay.

"But you said the sugar was in the can next to the flour," Katie accused.

Now it was Mother's turn to be flustered. It seemed that she'd had the can of sugar out for the peaches, so Katie had gotten the wrong can. Katie muttered about people who were so nicety-neat they had to keep laundry soap in a canister instead of leaving it in the soapbox where it belonged.

"Well, it's too bad, after all your work," Mother sympathized, "but maybe you can earn money some other way."

Katie's head came up. "Why, I'm not going to quit now," she said, surprised at Mother. "We'll just have to make more lemonade."

"Oh, Katie," Sue groaned. "I'm so hot and tired. Let's just give it up."

"Yes, honey," Mother said. "Try it some other day when you're fresh. It's almost time for lunch now."

"No," Katie said stubbornly. She'd made up her mind to sell lemonade today, and she was going to do it.

"Don't you see, Mother?" she pleaded. "We've already got the stand and the popcorn. It's such a good idea. We'll make it work this time."

"Oh dear," Mother sighed. "Well then, at least wait until you've had your lunch."

"No, right now. More people will be out at lunchtime."

"The popcorn!" Sue suddenly remembered.

She ran out to see if it was still there. Katie borrowed a quarter from Mother to buy more lemons, insisting she'd pay it back out of the lemonade profits. Sue came back with the bowl of popcorn, fortunately unharmed. Sighing deeply, she began to wash the lemonade pitcher, while Katie John set off once more for Flower's Grocery.

It was so hot out now that little shimmers came up from the white sidewalk. Katie walked slowly, wiping her red face. This time, *everything* would go right, she promised herself fiercely.

"Well, well," Mr. Flower beamed, wiping his hands on his apron. "Back for more lemons? Business good, hey?"

"No," Katie answered, her voice grim. "But it will be."

She wasn't going to tell him about the soapy lemonade,

but the beet-faced storekeeper was so nice about putting extra lemons in the sack that finally she did.

"Too bad, too bad," Mr. Flower sympathized. "But you stick to it, hey? Good girl!"

That made Katie feel a little better, and she ran back through the heat to her house.

Mother had made sandwiches for the girls to take out to the stand with them, and Sue had water and sugar ready in the pitcher. Wearily the girls squeezed lemons— cut and squeeze, cut and squeeze. They breathed heavily and worked silently, and they didn't worry about fishing out the stray lemon seeds. Add red food coloring, drop in ice cubes, stir it up. . . .

"Now!" Katie said. "Now we will sell lemonade."

"Oh, I hope so," Sue sighed. Her shoulders drooped, but she helped carry out the popcorn and lemonade once more.

Right away, here came a woman with a grocery sack. "I'll take a glass, dearie," she said to Katie. "Mm, that popcorn looks good."

She set down her sack with a puff, paid her nickel, and helped herself to popcorn. The girls watched anxiously as she drank from her glass and then breathed big sighs of relief as she declared, "Delicious!"

"See, I said it'd be all right now!" Katie said happily.

It was, too. People and more people kept coming— women with grocery sacks, men with grocery sacks, girls with grocery sacks, and even some big boys in a hotrod.

And they all bought lemonade. Money rattled into the box even after the popcorn was all gone.

The big lemonade pitcher was almost empty, too, when here came Mr. Flower without his apron.

"How about some lemonade, young lady?" he chuckled to Katie. "Just what I need to settle my lunch."

"Oh, it's been wonderful, Mr. Flower. Thirsty people all over the place," Katie chattered, as she poured the rest of the lemonade into a glass for him. "No," she pushed back his nickel, "we've got enough already."

"Good, good." The storekeeper smacked his lips over the lemonade. "I told everybody there was a lemonade stand down the street, run by a determined business-woman who made the best lemonade in the world."

He winked at Katie, and Katie blushed. So that was it. That's why all the people had grocery sacks. Anyway, they'd all liked their lemonade and popcorn.

"How would you like to make a business deal?" Mr. Flower was saying. "You run a lemonade stand every day, and I'll send folks down here. That way I sell you lots of lemons and we both profit. What say?"

Katie hesitated, and Sue shuddered. "No, Katie!" she begged.

Katie John laughed and shook her head. "Thanks a lot, Mr. Flower," she said. "But I've squeezed enough lemons to last me all summer."

The lemonade stand had been worth it, though. The next day after *Little Women,* Katie declared happily that she'd never cried so much at a movie in her life.

Aunt Emily's Story

The morning was growing darker instead of brighter. The sun had already been hot in the July sky when Katie had gotten up that morning, but black clouds were piling up. By ten o'clock the heat caught under the clouds seemed tight with waiting, and it was almost dark inside the old house

"We're going to have a regular old Midwestern thunder-and-lightning storm," Mother told Katie. "Quick, run and bring in the cushions from the lawn swing!"

Katie hurried out to the glider on the front lawn, gathered up the cushions, and stacked them on the front porch. A low rumble sounded up in the clouds, a sort of clearing of the throat.

Katie looked at the cushions. What better place to watch the show? Quickly she made a nest for herself. Back in California thunder-and-lightning storms were rare, and she'd never seen a really big one.

A brilliant line zigzagged across the clouds, followed

by a *cra-a-ck* that jerked Katie to her feet. Whew! She didn't know thunder was *that* loud. Maybe she should go into the house—but no, that was silly. Thunder couldn't hurt her. She made herself sit down again, even though she winced at every flash and crack. But it was exciting, too, as if the whole sky had suddenly gotten awfully mad about something.

Katie's breath came faster. The storm was reaching its peak—those clouds just *must* burst! Yes, there on the sidewalk was the first big splat of rain. Lone drops fell *spat, spat, spat*, then the rain came down in great streaks. The lightning and thunder rolled on across the river, and the show was over.

Well, that was something! Katie got up and went into the house. Now what should she do? Sue had gone with her mother to spend the day with an aunt in the country. And Katie didn't know any other children; this neighborhood was mostly big old houses with old people living in them.

Katie wandered into the parlor, picked up a little Chinese vase, looked at the figures on it, and set it down. She could dress up Lulu. But the cat didn't seem to be around. Probably out in the barn hunting mice. Mother was getting ready to go to the grocery store. Dad was upstairs working. She could hear his typewriter in the still house.

Upstairs. That reminded her. There was a back wing up there that she hadn't explored much. And what better time for exploring than a good, rainy day?

Katie ran up the stairs to the second floor, opened a door, and went down two steps to the back wing. She remembered now that one of these rooms had been Great-Aunt Emily's private sitting room when she was a girl. Mother had told her when she first showed Katie around the house.

She opened a door and peeked in. Yes, this was it. There was a pretty white marble fireplace and a little rocker. Glass doors opened onto a small balcony over-looking the vegetable garden. Did Aunt Emily ever stand on the balcony while a beau serenaded her from below, Katie wondered.

A movement in the vegetable garden caught her eye. It was Prince, Miss Crackenberry's horrid little dog, out there in the rain. Oh, that little beast! He was digging right in the middle of the tomato patch, tearing up the vines. Katie pulled open the balcony doors to shout at him, but he picked up a bone and trotted back to his own yard, waving that silly fluffy tail.

Katie stepped out onto the balcony, anyway, and pre-tended she was Aunt Emily being serenaded by a young man with a guitar. Surely Aunt Emily must have had beaux—Katie liked the old-fashioned word. Wonder why Aunt Emily had ended up an old maid. Was she awfully ugly?

Come to think of it, she didn't know much about Aunt Emily at all, except that Mother had loved her. Mother's mother had died when she was a little girl, so Mother had spent every summer with Aunt Emily. At first, Mother said, Grandpa—Aunt Emily's father—had lived here too, but then he'd died, and Aunt Emily had lived alone. For goodness' sakes, why had she stayed by herself in this big old house all those years?

Katie was getting wet, so she went back into the sitting room. Maybe there'd be a picture of Aunt Emily somewhere. Yes, over there on a stand was an old photograph in a curly iron frame. It showed a young woman in a long, high-waisted dress with great puffed sleeves. Katie looked on the back. On it was written: "Miss Emily Clark, 1898."

She studied the photograph. The girl was posed on the steps of this house. Why no, she wasn't ugly. Even in the faded picture, her eyes seemed to sparkle, and she looked eager. As if she were about to dash off the steps and away to something exciting.

She looks sort of like me, Katie thought suddenly.

But then, why hadn't she married, if she wasn't ugly? Well now, here was something to do. She'd just hunt around Aunt Emily's sitting room and see what she could find out about her.

There were sheets over some of the furniture. Katie peeked under the sheets until she found a desk. Just the thing. She unfolded the front lid that came down to form the writing stand. Inside were pigeonholes and many little shallow drawers. Katie settled happily to work.

She found silver cufflinks—whose?—buttons, a brooch, as well as pens, flowered stationery, and a bottle of dried ink. In one drawer was a program. "St. John's Episcopal Church, Benefit Chess Pageant," she read, "June 12, 1897." People had played the part of chess pieces, and Miss Emily Clark was the White Queen. Oh, the lovely things people did in the olden days!

In another drawer she found a sheaf of letters from a St. Louis department store, each ordering more of Aunt Emily's hand-painted, hand-laced doilies. My! Aunt Emily must have earned a lot of money for a woman in those days, making doilies. She must have been a good businesswoman, too, for in one letter the store agreed to pay the higher price she asked.

At last Katie John found a thin set of letters tied with a faded pink ribbon. The pages were yellow and brittle with age. But wait. Was it wrong to read someone else's letters? If these were my letters, Katie reasoned, I'd want my great-niece to read them, so she'd know what sort of person I was.

Carefully she unfolded the first page. It began: "My Dear Miss Emily." Katie looked at the signature—"Yr. Obdt. Servant and Faithful Friend, Robert Bugler." A man, maybe a beau!

She read: "We have arrived in Cuba and the weather is very warm. Soon we shall leave the ship to go to camp; but do not be alarmed, dear Emily, for we shall soon attend to these Spaniards."

Spaniards? Katie looked at the date, 1898. Why, he must have gone to fight in the Spanish-American War!

Let's see, that was in Cuba in 1898, and the Americans won. Would he tell about battles?

In the next letter Mr. Bugler was still on the ship. He wrote about the heat and said they'd had beef and beans to eat. There were seven or eight letters, but by the last one he still hadn't gotten off the ship. It was still hot and he was still having beef and beans for dinner.

Nevertheless, Katie John was sitting straight up with excitement, for the letters told one very important thing. Mr. Bugler was Aunt Emily's fiancé! They were engaged to be married, for he kept talking about the lovely wedding they'd have just as soon as he got back.

Then what had happened? Had poor Mr. Bugler been killed in the war?

Katie hunted through the desk, but found nothing more. A quick search around the room turned up some pretty ornaments, but nothing about Mr. Bugler. Where else could she look? There were some barrels of things in the basement and a trunk in the third-floor hall. Maybe in the trunk?

As Katie went into the main part of the house she saw Dad in the hallway below at the front door, letting in a fat man. He was probably a plumber. The pipes in the house were so old something was always springing a leak.

She ran upstairs to the third floor. Here the rooms were smaller, the ceiling lower, and the rain drummed loudly on the flat roof. How cozy it was up here in the top of the house.

At the end of the hall under a window stood the trunk,

piled high with old magazines. Katie took them off and stacked them on the floor. She lifted the trunk lid. Ah! Pasted inside the lid was a neat card, saying "Property of Emily C. Clark" and listing the address. Katie took out a dusty layer of old newspapers. And there were treasures for rainy-day browsing.

She saw shimmers of cloth, folded papers, books. Here, a dear little cream pitcher with the picture of a Dutch boy on its side. Here, a stack of Aunt Emily's doilies, with pictures and verses drawn on them in faded ink. But nothing about Mr. Bugler.

Katie took out that tray of the trunk. The bottom was filled with the sheen of white satin. Carefully she lifted it out. Oh-h, it was gorgeous! It was a dress, long and full, with deep borders of lace at the neckline. A piece of paper fluttered out of the folds of satin. Katie read the words on it: "My wedding gown."

Katie's throat felt tight. Oh, poor dear Aunt Emily. Here was her wedding dress, and she'd never worn it. What had happened?

There was nothing in the trunk to tell her more. Katie started to fold up the heavy satin, though she hated to bury it away again. It was so beautiful . . . would look so beautiful on. Did she dare put it on? Perhaps if she were very careful . . . Katie stepped out of her shorts and pulled off her blouse. With gentle fingers she opened the many tiny hooks on the gown. Slowly she eased the satin and lace over her head.

With a rich *swish*, the dress fell around her. Of course,

it was too long. When she had fastened the snaps, though, she found that it almost fitted at the waist.

"What a tiny waist she must have had," Katie marveled.

The top of the gown was much too full for Katie, but it was stiff with lace. She smoothed the lace with one finger, wondering if Aunt Emily had made it. Now, she wished to see herself in a mirror. Gathering up the skirt so that it wouldn't drag on the floor, she started for one of the bedrooms.

She stopped. Someone was coming up the stairs. It was Dad, bringing the fat man she'd seen downstairs.

Dad caught sight of her and snorted. "Well, Miss Kate, what are you up to?"

The fat man was puffing from the stairs. He winked at Katie and said, "Fancy duds you got, sis."

"I was looking through that old trunk," Katie began.

"Better not get into those things without asking your mother," Dad interrupted. He seemed in a hurry to get back to his business with the man. "Now on this floor, sir," he said, "we have four bedrooms and a bathroom."

Why, Dad was showing the house to this man. He must be a buyer. Katie John held up the skirt and hurried after them. She'd help Dad.

"There's a fireplace in every bedroom," she said.

"Fire hazards, sis," the man grunted, and to Katie's dismay he spit on a painted fire screen. "Roomers might set fire to the place."

"Roomers?" Katie faltered.

"Sure," the man said. "All an old rattletrap place like this is good for is a rooming house."

"But—"

"Katie John," Dad said firmly, "go into another room and take off that dress—now."

As Katie changed into her clothes she could hear the fat man across the hallway, opening closet doors and rapping on walls. He talked to Dad as if this house was an old hulk, and he seemed interested mainly in how many renters he could squeeze into the house. Great-Grandfather Clark would turn over in his grave, Katie thought. And Aunt Emily certainly hadn't kept up the old Clark place all these years for it to be turned into a cheap rooming house.

Katie John marched out to the fat man and smiled sweetly.

"There are lots of bathrooms, too," she said. "Six, you know. Of course, all the plumbing is old. But the pipes don't start leaking all at once, just sometimes. Except for that pipe in the second-floor hall," she chattered on, ignoring Dad, who was waving his hands and scowling at her from behind the man's back.

She laughed merrily. "Dad says *that* pipe should be solid gold, so much money has been spent repairing it."

"Hold it," the fat man growled. He turned to Dad. "Just how old is the plumbing?"

"Well, ah, naturally it's not new—ha ha." Dad didn't

look happy. "About fifty years old, I'd say. You can't expect an old house to have new plumbing."

"Hmph. I don't know," the man shook his head. "I don't want to spend a lot on repairs. Just want to make some money off the house for a few years before it falls apart. Guess I'll have to think it over some more."

He started down the stairs. Dad glared at Katie and followed him.

Katie felt as though she'd done a good deed. She'd saved the house from that man, she thought, as she folded the wedding gown back into the trunk. Aunt Emily must be glad, up in heaven.

When she ran downstairs the fat man was gone and Dad was telling Mother about what had happened.

"Miss Katherine certainly fixed that sale," he said. "We won't see any more of him—and he's the only interested buyer we've had."

"Oh, but, Daddy," Katie coaxed, "you wouldn't really let him turn it into a rooming house, would you? He was mean. He wouldn't love the house and take care of it."

Dad laughed ruefully. "Katie, selling a house isn't like giving away kittens. You may pick and choose for a good home for your kittens, but you don't try to pick a good owner for a home."

"This house you should," Katie insisted.

Mother smiled at her. "I feel rather the way Katie does. The Clark family has been happy in this house for almost ninety years. It seems a shame to turn the house over to someone who'd let it go to pieces."

That reminded Katie of Aunt Emily, and she told Mother of her search through Aunt Emily's things this morning. Dad was interested and followed along as Mother went back to the kitchen to put the groceries away.

"But what became of Mr. Bugler?" Katie asked. "Did he die in the war?"

Mother laughed. "No, he didn't die. He came back and Aunt Emily wouldn't have him, after all."

The story went that while Robert Bugler was at war he'd had a house built for himself and Aunt Emily to live in. But when he came back someone offered him a good bit of money for the house so he sold it. He told Aunt Emily they could just as easily live with his mother and father in their big house.

Aunt Emily was very strong-minded, Mother said. She told Robert that if she couldn't have a home of her own, she'd stay in this house. They quarreled, and stay she did.

"I don't blame her." Katie John sighed. "But how sad."

Mother laughed again. "I don't think it was, really. From what Aunt Emily told me, she was glad for the excuse to break the engagement. Robert Bugler wasn't as romantic-looking when he came back from the war as he was when he left. He was quite plump and rosy, from sitting on the ship, eating and eating. She said she never could abide fat men."

"All the more reason we shouldn't have sold the house to that man today," Katie said triumphantly.

"Actually, I think that she just found she didn't love Robert after all," Mother said. "A woman will put up with anything from a man she loves."

"Glad to hear it," Dad broke in. "Now that it's stopped raining, I'm going down to the river to fish. Will you clean the fish for me?"

"Oh—" Mother was caught. "All right! Maybe you won't catch anything, anyway."

"May I go with you, Dad?" Katie jumped up. "I'll make a lunch."

She still wasn't satisfied about Aunt Emily, though— about why she'd stayed alone in this big house all her life. Surely, if she was so strong-minded she could have gone adventuring into the world, been a teacher or something. Did she stay in the house because it had been in the family so long, and she couldn't bear to sell it to strangers?

I like the house, Katie decided, but that wouldn't be reason enough for me. She tucked away the thoughts and went off to the river with Dad.

The Fine Old Pioneer Bone

"I think little yellow tomatoes taste good because they look so darling," Sue said. She popped one into her mouth and hunted through the vines for more of the tiny tomatoes for her basket.

Sue and Katie John were out in the garden gathering vegetables for Katie's mother.

"I know," Katie said thoughtfully, as she picked pea pods. "It's like putting a little golden sun in your mouth. And then when you bite it, the whole tomato squishes at once."

The garden made her dreamy. It was such a wild place, with the green tansy and tall weeds tangled in among the rows of corn and the bean and pea vines that grew up around poles. Sort of a far-off place. Of course it was midsummer hot now, but the walnut trees swung patches of shade over the garden.

Katie split open a pea pod and scraped the row of little peas into her mouth. Then she ate the pod.

"I never knew until this summer that raw peas were good to eat," she told Sue. "They're so sweet and crisp, lots better than cooked ones. Even the pods are good."

"Look!" Sue interrupted.

A small brown rabbit hopped out of the weeds and disappeared by a walnut tree at the bottom of the garden.

"Then Mother was right." Katie jumped up. "She said a family of rabbits was living in a hole under that tree."

"Underneath the roots, just like Peter Rabbit." Sue was delighted.

Quietly the girls walked to the tree. There was a hole between the roots, sure enough. Katie John lay down on her stomach and tried to look down the hole, but she couldn't see anything.

"Let's dig down so we can see their house," she said.

"Oh, but that would ruin their tunnel," Sue protested.

Katie promised, "We'll put it all back just the same."

She began to dig at the soft dirt with her hands. It came out easily and she scooped it into a mound, to put back later. The hole was getting bigger. But now her fingers touched something hard. A rock, probably. It was in the way, and she pulled it out. It was white and—

"Why, it's a bone," Katie said.

This was no ordinary bone, of the sort buried by Prince. It was long and smooth, like the bone of an arm or a leg. Katie John dropped it quickly.

"Sue," she said in a hushed voice, "I think it's real! I mean, it's human—a people bone!"

Sue looked at the bone, half-frightened. "But how would a person's bone get here?"

"I just remembered!" Katie exclaimed. "It *is* a human bone. Because there used to be a cemetery here! Mother told me!"

Ever since she'd become so interested in Great-Aunt Emily, she explained to Sue, Mother had been telling her tales of Aunt Emily and the old house. One day Mother had mentioned that, before houses were built along this bluff, there had been a cemetery here.

"Right at this corner!" Katie said. "The first settlers were buried here, way back in the 1800's, before the Civil War."

When houses were about to be built here, Katie went on, all the coffins were moved to the new cemetery on the other side of town.

"But maybe they missed a few bones!" she ended.

The girls stared at the bone lying there in the dirt. Had it really belonged to a person once? Had somebody walked on that leg? What should they do with it?

"Let's put it back," Sue said.

"No, let's find out if it's really human."

"But how?"

Katie thought. Dad was writing, so she couldn't ask him. Mother was across the street helping a neighbor fit a dress—and she probably wouldn't know anyway.

"The library," Katie decided. "We'll ask at the library. Librarians are always answering questions."

The library was only two blocks away, and Katie John spent a lot of time there. Already one librarian in the children's room, a very old lady named Miss Squires, was her special friend. Yes, Miss Squires would surely help them find out about this bone.

"But—how will we get it to the library?" Sue hesitated. "Are you just going to carry it in your hand?"

"Oh no. That wouldn't seem respectful to the bone. Maybe we could carry it in a paper sack." Katie thought about it. "Though I don't think I'd like my bones carried around in a brown paper sack. In fact, I don't think I'd like my bones carried around at all."

"Let's just put it back," Sue begged.

"No." Katie John shook her head firmly. "We can't leave it here because Prince might dig it up."

"That's right!" Sue looked at Katie in horror.

"We'll just have to take it in a sack," Katie decided. "I'll get one from the kitchen."

"Don't forget your peas," Sue called after her, and then followed with both vegetable baskets.

After all, Katie put the bone in a box. That seemed more polite than bouncing the bone along in a sack. The box was too bulky to tuck under her arm, so she held it in front of her as she and Sue went down the street.

Even though it was only midmorning, the day was so hot that sweat stood on Katie's cheeks under her eyes. She could feel her hair straggling on her neck. Sue looked just as cool and calm as ever, though. Now why couldn't she have hair like Sue's? The heat just made it curl in little tendrils around her face. Oh well—Katie pushed her own hair back—hair wasn't important now. The bone was, and now they'd arrived at the library.

The main floor of the library was reached by wide stairs inside. Down the stairs, along with the storerooms, was the children's department. It was lots cooler inside, and quiet. Miss Squires was alone in the children's room, reading. It was a children's book, Katie could tell from the cover.

Katie wondered if she should ask Miss Squires about the bone after all. Miss Squires had feathery white curls across her forehead and a chirpy voice, and she could always find you a good book when you weren't sure what you wanted. But she wasn't much for knowing about science and bones and things like that. Still, she might know how to find out.

"Oh, girls!" Miss Squires looked up. "You're just the ones who'd love this book. It's *One Foot in Fairyland,* and I don't know how I missed it before. Listen." She read a paragraph from the book.

"I'd like to take it when you're done with it, Miss Squires," Sue said.

"Me too," Katie added, "but right now we want to ask you something. We want to know what this is." She opened the box.

Miss Squires peered in. "Why, it's a bone," she decided.

"I know, but what kind?" Katie said. "I mean, is it

a human bone?" She explained how she and Sue had found it, and about the old cemetery.

"Oh dear!" Miss Squires drew back from the bone. "Oh my, I don't know, girls. It does look like a leg bone, doesn't it? Now let's see." She tapped her pencil against her forehead curls as she thought.

"Yes," she said finally. "We'll look in the big anatomy book upstairs. It has pictures of all the bones in the body."

She couldn't leave the children's department untended, though, so it was decided that Sue would stay down here, in charge while Miss Squires was gone. That suited Sue just fine. She didn't care much for keeping constant company with that bone anyway.

Katie followed Miss Squires up the wide staircase, feeling quite important. Back in California, the library rooms, both children and adult, were right next to each other. But Barton's Bluff was an old-fashioned town and this was an old-fashioned library, and here children weren't usually allowed upstairs in the main library. She'd been upstairs once before with her dad, but now she had a grown-up errand of her own up here.

Miss Squires led her to a great red wooden rocking chair. "Now you wait here, Katie John," she told her, "while I find the anatomy book."

Katie sat on the edge of the chair, so that her feet would still touch the floor. For goodness' sakes, who was big enough to fit comfortably in this chair? She held the box in her lap and looked around.

The big reading room was warm and quiet; the few

people in it were grown-ups and serious. One man was reading fine print in a newspaper with a magnifying glass, and another man was reading a huge book and writing notes on a paper. The rows and rows of bookshelves were beyond the long desk where people checked out books. A gray-haired librarian sat at this desk, as though guarding the books behind her.

Just then there was a scrabbling noise on the stairs, and the sound of someone muttering. There appeared little Miss Crackenberry, with Prince tugging ahead on his leash, his toenails clicking on the steps.

"—Stairs to climb!" Katie heard her puffing. "Main library should be on the ground floor, let the children climb!"

Katie John slid back out of sight into the chair and watched as Miss Crackenberry trotted over to the desk and emptied her satchelful of books on the counter. The librarian frowned over the desk at Prince, who snarled back.

"Oh, Miss Crackenberry," the librarian said. "You know we've asked you not to bring Prince into the library." She lowered her voice. "He might—ah—forget where he is—"

"Prince *never* lifts his leg in public!" Miss Crackenberry said clearly. "Come, Prince."

She went around the desk, back toward the bookshelves, and the librarian stood aside to give Prince room.

Katie scowled after them. That old Miss Crackenberry

and Prince always got their way. Sometimes it seemed as if the meaner people were, the more they got their own way. Well, someday, she promised herself, maybe someday . . .

She settled back to waiting for Miss Squires. Covering the wall opposite her was a large picture of the Missouri soldiers returning from the Civil War. It was bronze-colored and done in some kind of carving that made the figures stand out.

Just think. That was almost one hundred years ago, yet this bone was already buried when it happened. This person had never known about the war that was coming. That is, if this *was* a person's bone.

Katie opened the box to look at the bone again. She'd never seen a human bone before, so it was hard to tell if it looked one hundred years old.

There was a click on the floor, a snuffle, and there was Prince, sticking his nose into the box.

"Shoo! Go away!" Katie snatched the bone up high.

Prince's leash trailed behind him, and Miss Crackenberry was nowhere in sight. He growled at Katie and hopped on his short hind legs, trying to reach the bone.

"Oh, shame!" Katie cried. She kicked at the dog.

"Here! Stop that! Stop kicking that dog!" Miss Crackenberry rushed out from the bookshelves.

"Well, he's trying to get this bone!" Katie said hotly. "Do you want your dog chewing on a real human bone?"

"What's that, young lady?"

Still holding the bone high while Prince jumped at it, Katie told about finding the bone and about the cemetery. A wicked idea came to her.

She added pointedly, "All our garden used to be a cemetery. The vegetable garden too, where Prince keeps digging up bones and burying them."

Miss Crackenberry's face got red. "He's been digging up bones where—" She snapped her mouth shut and grabbed Prince's leash. "Come, you bad dog!" She jerked him back toward the bookshelves.

Katie snickered as she put the bone back into the box. Now maybe old Miss Crackenberry would think twice about letting her dog dig up their vegetable garden!

Miss Squires came hurrying up with a large book in her arms. "Here we are, Katie. And I think, yes, I do believe—well, look at this picture."

She put the book in Katie's lap, and they bent their heads over a drawing in the book. It showed human leg bones, both the upper and lower parts. Katie held up her bone, looking from it to the picture.

"Oh, Miss Squires," she said slowly, "it looks like it. Oh my!" Thoughts raced through her mind, such as: here she was, holding a human bone, and would there be an official burying ceremony at the cemetery now, and would they have her bury this fine old pioneer bone?

"But right here, it doesn't look quite like the picture," she noticed. "Is there a drawing with a different view?"

She turned the page. There was another drawing of a leg bone.

"Oh, yes!" Katie cried certainly. "Now this looks exactly like the bone."

"Yes, yes," Miss Squires agreed.

"But—oh!" Katie read the words under the drawing. "But this is—this drawing is of a horse's leg!"

Katie stared at the bone, then back at the drawing. There was no mistake. The shape of the bone was just like the drawing.

"A horse's leg!" she said in dismay. "Nothing but an old horse bone! Oh fiddle!"

She dropped the bone into the box on the floor and snapped the anatomy book shut. She should have known it wouldn't be anything exciting. Just a dull old horse bone.

"I'm sorry I bothered you about a horse bone," she told Miss Squires.

Miss Squires smiled. "Well, well, dear. I know you're disappointed. But isn't it better to know that you don't have pioneer bones in your garden? The pioneer souls are in heaven, and all the pioneer bones are safely at rest in the cemetery where they belong."

"Oh, yes, I'm glad," Katie said glumly.

There was a scuffle by her feet. Katie looked down and saw Prince darting across the room toward the stairs, his leash trailing. In his mouth was the bone.

"Hey!" Katie called out, forgetting all about silence in the library. "Come back with that bone!"

She jumped up and started after him, trying to step on the leash to stop him. At the sound of commotion, Miss

Crackenberry flurried out with an armload of books.

"What? What?" she cried.

She saw Prince. She saw the bone in his mouth. Miss Crackenberry's arms flew up and the books scattered to the floor.

"Prince!" she screamed in horror. "Oh, you mustn't! No, no!" She flew after the little dog as he tore down the stairway.

Katie and the people in the reading room could hear her crying, "Stop, stop! No, no!" all the way down and out into the street.

"Well!" Katie burst out laughing.

"But why did she make such a fuss?" Miss Squires wondered.

"Don't you see?" Katie gasped in delight. "She thinks —she thinks he's got a human bone!"

"Why, how dreadful!" said Miss Squires. "The poor woman!"

"Oh, yes, it's dreadful!" Katie said through bubbles of giggles.

And I'll bet she never lets Prince dig up our garden again, she told herself happily. A warm, satisfied feeling spread through her. So! Meanness didn't always sail freely through the world. For once, meanness—Prince's and Miss Crackenberry's—had gotten just what it deserved.

Katie felt so good about it that she didn't even hate Miss Crackenberry any more. She began picking up the books scattered on the floor.

"I'll take these along to Miss Crackenberry," she said generously. "I'll explain about the bone, though I'm afraid she's already had the worst shock."

Then she started to giggle, all over again. Sue must be downstairs wondering what all the noise was about. Wait 'til she told Sue all about it!

The Covered Bridge

"I thought Barton's Bluff was a sleepy country town until I saw John's Landing," Katie told Sue. "Why, it's only got one street, and there's a tree growing right out in the middle of it."

They were sitting on Sue's front steps, and Katie was telling about her morning's trip. She and Dad had driven down into the country to get a bushel of tomatoes for canning. On the way they'd taken a side road through John's Landing.

"I know," Sue said. "It's a famous tree. That's why they don't cut it down."

"Maybe somebody was hanged there!"

"Oh, Katie, you're always getting excited," Sue said, smoothing her wide skirt out over her feet. "I think it's famous because the first settler planted it, or something like that."

"Oh well." Katie settled back. It was too hot to get

excited anyway. "Probably they don't need to cut it down because there's no traffic."

She'd liked John's Landing, though, drowsing there in the sun by the river. Once the Mississippi steamboats had stopped there, Dad said, but now there were just a few homes of people who lived there because their families always had. The town had one dusty street, a little red brick post office, and a general store with a wooden porch. When she and Dad had driven through, the only people they saw were two men sitting on the store's porch. Some long hound dogs had been asleep in the street, in the tree's shade, and when Dad had honked the horn at them they'd gotten up very slowly.

"I'd like to go back there sometime," Katie John said. "And oh, there was another darling little side road I wanted to explore, but Dad said we didn't have time."

"Where was that?"

Outside of Barton's Bluff, just before the Possum River bridge, she explained. It was just a grassy lane that had curved in among thick trees. It had looked so pretty back in there, and she had seen what looked like an old gray barn roof.

"Why, that's the covered bridge," Sue said, "on the old road to John's Landing."

"Covered bridge!" Katie cried. "I've never seen a covered bridge."

Between Barton's Bluff and John's Landing, the little Possum River emptied into the Mississippi. Long ago,

Sue said, the way to John's Landing crossed the Possum River through the covered bridge—a structure with side walls and barnlike roof to protect it from the weather. But the bridge had grown old and dangerous. A new bridge had been built and a new road laid that by-passed forgotten little John's Landing.

"You can still walk through the bridge, though," Sue said. "It's sort of scary, because it's like a dark tunnel, but it's fun to holler inside and hear your echo. And just on the other side of the bridge is a whole bunch of huckleberry bushes, the best berries around here."

"Ohh," Katie sighed. "I knew we should have explored that road. Fiddle. Now Dad will probably never get back that way."

"Why wait for your dad to take you?" Sue said. "I will. We can ride bikes."

Katie stared at her plump friend. Usually she, Katie, did all the leading. Now here was Sue, calmly suggesting they go adventuring out into the country all by themselves.

"It's all right." Sue laughed at Katie's expression. "The kids around here ride bikes to the woods a lot. I used to go with my sister, Janet, but now she's fifteen she thinks she's too grown up."

Katie John didn't have a bicycle, but Sue said it would be all right for her to ride Janet's old one. Katie ran home to tell Mother where they were going, and Mother gave her some cookies for her pocket. Then the girls set off.

As they rode down the street, Katie tried to explain why she hadn't thought of this adventure. Back home in California—for California was still home, even if they were moving to New York—she'd lived in the sunny central valley of the state, which had once been almost a desert. There, if she'd ridden a bike outside of town, she'd have come to field upon field of vegetables or cotton, watered by irrigation ditches. And where the fields weren't watered, there was nothing but bare dirt or dusty weeds—no little brooks or clumps of woods or grassy lanes. When she and her folks wanted to go to the country they had to drive two hours, up into the mountains, before they found many trees or streams.

"You're lucky, being able to go to the woods any time you want to, without waiting for your folks," Katie told Sue.

Surprising Sue, who'd always seemed interested only in dolls, said, "I'd hate to be cooped up in a town all the time."

Presently Sue said, "Turn down this street."

"But the road out of town goes that way."

"Yes, but I know a boy who lives down this way," Sue said, and kept on pedaling.

"You're not going to take a boy with us, are you?"

"No." Sue looked flustered. "I just want to ride past his house."

"But why—?"

"Sh! There he is! Don't say anything!" Sue put her

face down and pedaled her bike as if she didn't see the boy.

Katie looked at him, though, and saw an ordinary boy with brown hair and blue jeans. He was mowing a lawn.

"Quit looking at him," Sue murmured.

Just then the boy noticed the girls. "Hi, Sue," he called.

Sue turned with a very surprised look on her face and slowed her bicycle. "Oh, hi, Bob. Do you live around here?"

Katie stared at her in amazement.

"Right here," the boy said. "Where are you going?"

"Out to the old covered bridge. 'Bye now." Sue stood up and pumped her bicycle away quickly.

Katie followed on hers. "What's your hurry? And why'd you pretend you didn't know he lived there? Who is he, anyway?"

"He's going to be my boy friend at school next winter," Sue said. "I didn't want to look as though I was chasing him."

"Boy friend!" Katie John exclaimed. "Boys are dumb!"

She shook her head in disgust. She hadn't thought Sue would be silly over boys. Riding by a boy's house and then not even staying to talk to him, for goodness' sakes! Katie hoped she'd never get that crazy.

Now they'd passed the unpaved streets at the edge of town and were out into the country. The road went mostly downhill toward the Possum River, yet Katie was becoming quite breathless. The hot August sun had softened the tar on the road until it gave slightly under the bicycle tires, and the green woods that had looked so cool this morning now steamed like a jungle. Katie was used to the blazing dry heat of central California, but not this air that closed around her like a hot washrag.

"Let's stop and rest," she gasped.

"Sure." Sue wiped at the damp curls around her forehead.

They dropped their bikes and flopped on the grass under a big tree. Surprisingly, the earth under the grass was still cool and damp. Katie burrowed her hands beneath the grass to feel it. The barest breeze stirred the tree and cooled her head. Katie John rolled onto her back and closed her eyes. Spots of sunshine and shadow flickered on her eyelids.

"Sue," she said slowly, "did you ever wish you were famous?"

Sue was trying to split a grass blade for a whistle. "Hm-um. Never thought about it."

"I do," Katie John confessed. "I got to counting up one time, and only about fifty people in this whole world know me. I wish I could do something great and wonderful so that a thousand people would know me."

She leaned up on one elbow. "Does that sound conceited? I mean, I'm not stuck on myself. It's just that—" She sat up and sighed, because she couldn't say just what she meant.

Sue smiled at her. "Katie John, I know you're not stuck on yourself. I wouldn't want to be famous, myself, but maybe someday you will do something great and wonderful. Me, I'd rather just a few people liked me a lot."

Katie felt a rush of love for her friend. Sue was such a sweet girl. Of course it would be nicer to have a few people love you than have a thousand people just know about you. And yet . . .

She hugged Sue's shoulders and then turned to her bike in embarrassment. "Let's get going," she said. "I can hardly wait to taste those berries."

Soon they came to the turn-off, the old road to John's Landing. Katie could see the gray roof of the covered bridge, and, even though she knew what it was, it looked mysterious. Just think, an old covered bridge hidden back in the woods, as wonderful as finding a haunted house. Just off the road stood a sign with the paint flaking off. It read: "Bridge Condemned."

"Don't worry about that," Sue said. "That sign's been there ever since I can remember. Nobody pays any attention to it."

On the highway few cars had passed them in the hot afternoon. Now as their bicycles bumped along the grassy ruts the hush of the woods was complete. Up in the trees, looped thick with vines, birds called and twittered, yet their songs were a part of the hush.

Katie thought of the berries, hanging dark and plump on the bushes beyond the bridge. She could hardly wait to pop them into her dry mouth. Then the lane turned through the trees, and there stood the bridge.

"Oh, what a dear beautiful bridge!" Katie cried.

Its weathered gray boards were smooth with time, and vines had spread over its sides. Now that the bridge was no longer used, it had settled down to being simply part of the woods. Tree branches brushed the roof where it arched, and the grassy road ran into the old bridge's dark mouth. Through the bushes beside the bridge, Katie could see the flash of the little Possum River, as it rushed to join the Mississippi.

Katie and Sue got off their bikes and ran into the shadowy tunnel. The floorboards creaked but seemed to hold all right.

"Hello!" Katie shouted. "Hel-loo!" came a hollow echo.

"Hey, that's a wonderful echo," Katie said. "Ko-o," the bridge answered faithfully.

"Katie" "Sue" "Hi!" "Hellooo," the girls called. And "Aty" "Ooo" "Hi!" "Helloooo," the bridge hooted back.

Then came a different shout. "Hello yourself!"

The girls started and stared at each other. "Hey there!" the shout came again. It sounded from the road.

"Why, that's Bob's voice!" Sue said. "He's followed us."

She tried to frown, but her mouth went into a silly smile. Katie looked at her in disgust.

"Now look what you've done," she said. "You wanted him to follow us, didn't you?"

Then she giggled at a sudden idea. "I know! Let's give him a scare. Hurry, go hide in the huckleberry bushes."

She gave Sue a little push. Sue hesitated, but ran to obey Katie, as usual. Katie looked around for a place to hide. Ah. There was a post going up to the roof. It stood out from the wall just enough. It was a tight squeeze, but Katie managed to wedge herself between the post and the wall.

She could hear Bob's bicycle rattling now. "Where are you?" he called. "I see your bikes."

He laid his bike down and started into the bridge. His footsteps thumped and echoed.

"Oooo," Katie began softly, letting the moan grow louder and louder. The echo took it up, "OOOOOO." The sound of footsteps stopped.

"Cut it out," Bob said. "I know it's you girls." But he walked softly and slowly now.

Just as he passed her in the shadows, Katie yelled, "Boo!" and twisted to jump out at him.

However, there seemed to be some difficulty.

Such as not being able to get out.

She was stuck. Wedged tight as a cork in a bottle, between the post and the wall. Her twisting had done it.

"What's the matter, ghost, are you stuck?" Bob laughed. "Here." He hauled at her arm, but she didn't pop out.

Sue came running. "Hi, Bob. What's wrong, Katie?"

"Oh, I'm caught somehow," Katie muttered, embarrassed. "Get behind me and push while Bob pulls."

The pushing and pulling didn't help, though. Katie seemed to be caught at the hips.

"Oh, Katie, you're always getting stuck," Sue giggled. "This is worse than the time you got your finger stuck in the speaking tube hole."

"For a skinny girl, you sure are in there tight," Bob said, grinning.

They hauled and heaved until Katie's sides were sore. She tried to wiggle. She tried to scootch up or down. Nothing helped. She was just plain stuck.

"Maybe we'd better go for help." Sue began to worry.

"Maybe we'll have to get someone to chop the post down."

"Maybe they'll have to take the whole bridge apart to get you out." Bob laughed. "I can see it in the newspaper now: 'Katie John Tucker finally brings down the old covered bridge'!"

Sue giggled at Bob's wit. "Yes, Katie, then you'd be famous, the way you wanted."

"It's not funny," Katie snapped.

She could just picture what would happen if Sue went for help—the fire truck roaring out here with chisels and saws and ladders, maybe a police car too, people jumping in their cars to see the excitement, kids following on their bikes. The whole crowd would gawk and laugh while someone took the bridge apart from around her. Good heavens!

"You're not going to get anybody!" she cried. "Pull some more."

This certainly was worse than having her finger stuck. Then it had been simple for Mother to soap the finger. Here she'd need a whole washtub full of soapy water. Hmmm.

"Quit jerking my arms," she said ungratefully. "I've got an idea. Get gobs of mud from the riverbank and plaster me with it. Maybe I can slime my way out."

Sue and Bob stared at her and then ran out of the bridge, snickering.

Katie squirmed. She wasn't going to enjoy this. And

what would Mother say at the looks of her clothes? Still—

Sue and the boy came running back with handfuls of dripping mud. They plastered it all over Katie at the stuck points and ran for more. It was cold and she could feel it oozing next to her skin. It smelled of fish, too.

In their haste Sue and Bob managed to get mud splattered all over her, but Katie could hardly object under the circumstances. With the mud trickling down her sides, Katie gave one mighty twist. That did it. She staggered out of her slot, dripping river slime.

"Thank goodness," Sue cried.

"Too bad, Katie," Bob teased. "Now you won't get your name in the paper. Of course, we could sort of tell it around, what a good idea you had to ooze loose."

"Don't either of you ever tell a single soul!" Katie gasped, wiping the mud from her face.

Sue and Bob couldn't help laughing, and finally Katie had to join in, too. They hooted and hollered, and the more they laughed, the funnier it all seemed. And the echo joined in, until the old bridge shouted with laughter in the hot afternoon.

Katie John's Bad Day

The summer was growing old. A cool breeze was blowing this morning and leaves were rattling down from the trees. There was a feeling of lateness in the air. Soon it would be autumn and school would start. Katie John was glad, because she was getting tired of summer vacation. The only trouble was, no one had bought the house yet, and it looked as though she might have to start school right here in Barton's Bluff instead of in New York.

Well, school here, school there, she'd be glad to get back to work. Then Katie had an idea. Why not start a newspaper? A neighborhood newspaper that she and Sue could write and sell.

Sue thought it was a fine idea, too, so the girls set to work in Katie's bedroom. Her dad loaned them his second-best typewriter so they could type up their newspaper and make it look professional.

"Now you stay here and write fashion notes about new

fall clothes, Sue," Katie arranged things, "while I go out and get some ads. I'll try to find a good scoop for our front-page story."

On her way back from getting a real estate ad from Mr. Follensbee, Katie saw a moving van in the Bancrofts' driveway. That's right, they were moving. She got all the information and rushed to the "newspaper office."

"Scoop!" she cried. "I've got the front-page story! All about the Bancrofts' moving, and where they're going and everything."

Sue was busy at the typewriter, hunting and pecking as fast as she could.

"Wait!" she said, her face beaming. "I've already got the front-page story. A fire!"

"Where?"

"In your father's wastebasket. You should have been here, Katie John," Sue said in excitement. "It blazed all up the side of his desk and burned a hole in the rug, and your mother spilled a bucket of water all over his papers. All the yelling, my!"

Katie stood there. Here she'd missed all the excitement and Sue was writing the big front-page story for their first newspaper. That wasn't right because, she, Katie, was supposed to be the editor and Sue was just the helper, to write fashion news and the other dull things. It wasn't fair. After all, the newspaper was her idea.

"I don't think that should be the front-page story," Katie said flatly. "The fact that the Bancrofts are moving is important to a lot more people in the neighborhood than a little old wastebasket fire."

Sue stared at her. "But a fire is always big news," she insisted. "Besides, everybody knew the Bancrofts were going to move."

"I don't care!" Katie angrily thrust her fingers up through her bangs. "I'm the editor, and my father used to be a newspaper reporter, and I certainly ought to know what's news!"

"You're just jealous because my story is bigger than yours," Sue said hotly. "You always want to be the big shot!"

"I do not!" Katie yelled, and suddenly she hated Sue's fat face. Before she could stop it, her hand flew out and slapped Sue flat on the cheek.

"Oh!" both girls gasped.

Tears filled Sue's eyes. "All right for you, Katie John Tucker," she choked, and she ran out of the room, out of the house, down the street.

Katie's heart was pounding and her hand tingled, but she set her lips firmly. "I don't care," she muttered. "Served her right."

She tore Sue's paper out of the typewriter and crumpled it up. Rolling in a clean sheet, she began pecking out, "It is with deep regret that the neighborhood learns that the Bancrofts are moving to—" No, that wasn't right, because the neighborhood wasn't just learning about it. She started again, then sat back.

Wonder if Dad got burned? But she was right, a waste-basket fire wasn't a big story. It wasn't as if there'd been fire engines or sirens. Oh fiddle, she didn't want to make the newspaper after all. No fun alone. Stupid old Sue, spoiling everything.

Katie quit thinking, got up, and slammed out of the house. She wandered up the street toward the bluff. Now she'd have to give Mr. Follensbee his nickel back if there wasn't any newspaper or ad.

She was above the jungle on the bluff when the sound of shouting stopped her. Looking down, she saw children playing among the trees. Those were the tough kids from the river shacks, the ones Sue said they weren't supposed to play with.

A big girl with a mass of black hair was bossing some younger boys and girls, who were barefooted and smudgy. There was a boy about Katie's age, too. They had a blanket tent strung over a line between two trees, and they looked as though they were having a wonderful time. Katie headed down the hillside.

"Hi," she called to the big girl. "Can I play?"

The girl turned, her long hair whirling, and put her hands on her hips. "Who are you?"

"Why, I'm Katie Tucker."

"Are you chicken?" the girl demanded, and, as Katie looked puzzled, she added, "Chicken—scaredy-cat."

Katie lifted her chin. "Of course not. Are you?"

The girl's black eyes looked fierce in her brown face, then she grinned. "Everybody knows I'm not. Okay, you're all right. I'm Rita Baker, and these are my little brothers and sisters. That there," she pointed to the boy Katie's size, "he's Pete, that lives down my way, and his kid brother, Joey."

"Hi," Katie said.

"Okay now," Rita said. "We're going to play Indians and settlers. Katie, you can be the leader of the settlers and take Joey in the tent with you. Pete and the rest of us kids will be Indians. I'm Chief."

"No, I am," Pete said.

Rita's black eyes flashed. "Shut up. I already *said*."

Pete muttered but followed Rita off into the bushes, while Katie went into the tent with Joey. She wasn't just sure she liked being bossed around by this girl. Being the Indians would be more fun. Still, there was something wild and exciting about Rita that Katie liked.

Rita came running back. "Hey, build a fire in front of your tent. Here's some matches."

Dad had never let her play with matches, but finally Katie got the match lit and touched it to the sticks Joey had gathered. They crouched by the fire, pretending not to know that the Indians were sneaking up on them. In the attack the fire got scattered and the corner of the blanket tent was burned, but they got the fire put out.

"That's my mother's blanket," Pete said angrily. "It's all your fault," he told Rita.

"Shut up." She scowled.

"Make me!"

Rita rushed at him and scratched at his face. Pete

promptly punched her in the stomach. Rita sat down hard, screaming, "Get out of here, you—" Her face twisted in an ugly shape.

"Who wants to stay?" Pete jeered. "Who wants to play with a bunch of girls and babies?" He grabbed the blanket and Joey's hand. "Come on."

Pete and Joey ran away. Katie looked after them in dismay and then at Rita, still hunched over. Maybe she shouldn't get mixed up with these tough kids. They sure acted mean. She started toward the path up the hill.

But Rita threw her hair back and laughed. "Now they're gone we can really have some fun. Say, let's go swing on grapevines."

Katie hesitated. "How do you do that?"

Rita explained about the long wild grapevines that grew in the trees along the river.

"They're like long ropes and you can swing way out on them," she said. "And we've got some potatoes. After we play I'll show you how to roast potatoes outdoors."

Katie was enchanted all over again. "All right, let's go!"

With the little children following, Rita led the way along the hillside. They walked quite a way through the jungle until they came out by the bridge across the Mississippi. It seemed that the grapevines were across the river. They'd go over on the bridge.

"I don't think I should go so far from home," Katie said. "Maybe I'd better go ask my folks."

She knew what they'd say, though. They wouldn't let her go.

"I thought you said you weren't chicken!"

"I'm not. It's just that—" But the hot "I don't care" feeling she'd gotten from her fight with Sue was still with her. "All right. Why not? We'll be back soon." And she ran ahead toward the bridge.

Just then a pickup truck came along.

"Hey, mister," Rita called. "Can we ride to the other end of the bridge?"

"Sure, hop in," the man said.

Rita and the little ones jumped up into the open back of the truck. Katie stood hesitating. Something in her stomach stirred queasily. But at last she climbed in.

"Boy, this is living," Rita cried, as the truck started up and her hair streamed back in the wind.

Far below, little white-capped waves danced in the breeze, and Katie could look way down the river to where it curved through the hills. She put her face up to the fresh river air and breathed it in. It was good to be heading toward who-knows-what.

At the other end of the bridge the truck stopped and the children jumped out.

"Thank you!" Katie called.

There was no town on this side of the river, and the woods came right down to the sandy shores. Except for the road, Katie thought, this side of the river looked just as it must have when the Indians lived here. She ran down to the water's edge and looked across the river. There was Barton's Bluff, looking so tiny on the hills over there. It seemed covered with trees, with only a few rooftops and the church spire sticking out. That open space was Main Street, coming down to the waterfront.

"Now then," she turned to Rita, "where are the grape-vine swings?"

"We have to walk down the shore a ways," Rita said.

They set off, with the little children straggling behind, darting about finding mussel shells. Katie took off her shoes and felt the delicious crunch of warm sand under her feet.

"Ah!" she said happily. "What a glorious day!"

"Here." Rita handed her a small sack. "You carry the potatoes awhile."

They walked and walked, on down the riverbank. Once they came to a swampy place where a small stream ran into the river. Rita warned Katie to watch out for snakes, and Katie stepped gingerly through the mud.

At last Katie said, "Where are those grapevines? You didn't say it was so far."

"You didn't ask," Rita answered rudely. "Anytime you want to go back, go right ahead."

Katie muttered that she hadn't said anything about going back. Rita certainly was touchy, as if she liked picking fights. Katie wasn't sure she liked Rita after all.

Presently she saw a set of wooden planks floating at the water's edge. It was some kind of small barge or dock, anchored by a rope going down into the water.

"Say, let's sit out there and pretend we're on a raft going down the Mississippi," Katie said.

"Okay."

Katie started to wade into the water, then stopped. The bank dropped sharply under her feet. She staggered back. Maybe she'd better find out how deep it was there. She ran to the edge of the trees and found a good long stick. Stretching her arm over the water as far as she could, she thrust the stick down. It went clear down, the length of the stick, and she still hadn't touched bottom.

"My! It's really deep here," she said. "We can't wade out."

"Maybe we could jump," Rita suggested.

The raft floated so near that Katie could touch it with the stick. It was frustrating to have the raft so close and not be able to get on it. She studied the distance from shore to raft.

"It's pretty wide," she said.

"Go ahead, try it," Rita urged. "If you make it, I'll jump too."

"Yes, and what if I don't!"

Katie wasn't a very good swimmer yet. Besides, the raft was narrow. In jumping she might go on over the other side.

"You're chicken!" Rita said. "I dare you!"

"I am not. Darers go first."

"No, it was your idea," Rita insisted. "If you aren't chicken, prove it."

"All right, I will!" Katie cried. "You're just scared to go first, yourself."

She backed up on the shore, ran, and leaped high across the water. And landed on the raft. She sprawled down to keep from rolling on over its side.

"There! I made it!" she yelled. "Now who's chicken?"

Then her triumph turned to dismay. For now the distance between raft and shore was quite a bit wider. The force of her landing had thrust the raft farther out into the river.

"Now you've done it," Rita grinned. "How're you going to get back?"

Katie stared across the brown water that rocked between her and the shore. It was too far to jump. She'd barely made it before.

Oh, this was crazy. Here she was right by the shore, yet just too far to get back. Of course, she wasn't in any danger of floating off down the river, for the raft was anchored by the rope.

"The rope!" Katie said. "That's it. You kids haul in the rope and pull me back."

The steel cable was fastened to a rock just offshore. Rita waded in and reached down. She pulled, but nothing happened.

"Oh, the raft's too heavy. I can't move it," Rita said,

giving up. "Come on, Katie, swim back. Your clothes will dry off."

"But I can't swim very well," Katie objected. "The current might get me."

"Oh, come on."

Katie looked down at the muddy water. "No."

Rita shrugged. "Well, swim back or stay there. I can't wait around all day."

"You're not going to just go off and leave me?" Katie cried, shocked.

"What do you want us to do, sit here and look at you?" Rita's voice was hard. "We want to get down to the grapevine swings, don't we, kids?"

The little ones nodded, staring at Katie John.

"But what—" Katie stammered.

"Oh, quit being so chicken," Rita said, starting off. "Probably the raft will drift back pretty soon. Come on when you get back to shore."

Katie watched as Rita walked on down the riverbank, with the little Bakers trailing after her. So! She dares me into this mess, Katie thought bitterly, and then she just walks off and leaves me.

Now the shore was deserted, the woods standing silent. Katie looked across the river to Barton's Bluff, distant as a dream. Not a towboat, not a rowboat, no one in sight. She was entirely alone on the broad surface of the river. The sunshine seemed brown and old. It must be way past noon.

She was really going to catch it when she got home. Her folks had been pretty easy on her this summer because of the move. But this—Katie's stomach squirmed.

She just had to get off this raft. She'd have to swim. It was such a short way, really. And she could swim a little. Katie put one foot out toward the water. And then drew it back. Wait. Not yet.

She crouched on the splintery boards and looked at the water, cloudy with mud. What was down in it? If she swam would she touch fish, eels like the one she'd caught when she went fishing with Dad? Katie John shuddered, and then she couldn't stop trembling. Jump in, she thought. I can't. Jump. Her hands were sweating and she hardly breathed, staring at the water.

"Oh," she asked herself, "how did I ever get into this mess?"

But she knew. "Headstrong," she could hear Miss Crackenberry saying through her thin smile. She was, too. It had all started when she'd been so bound-determined to have her own way about the newspaper.

Tears burned Katie's eyes. She didn't want to think about Sue, but she couldn't help remembering how she'd slapped Sue. And how Sue had looked.

Sue is my good, loyal friend, and I hit her just because I wanted my own way.

Katie John bit her lip as hard as she could, to punish herself. Oh, if she ever got off here, she'd go straight to Sue. She'd get right down on her knees and tell Sue she could write the whole paper. And they'd play dolls whenever Sue wanted to.

She just had to go to Sue right now. Before she could hesitate, Katie threw herself forward.

I should have taken off my shoes, she remembered too late as the water rushed into her nose. Now she didn't worry about eels. She was busy just trying to kick her legs somehow. She couldn't get her arms and legs to going together. But at least she was moving.

Now the riverbank was closer. Katie let down a foot. It touched nothing. Oh, she was sinking! She flung out her arms, paddling again. And now, now her feet touched mud. Gasping, Katie heaved herself forward onto the sand and lay there.

I made it! I made it!

Suddenly she thought: What if Sue won't forgive me? But she knew Sue would. She's gooder than I am, Katie thought humbly.

She heard voices. There came Rita and the little Bakers.

"You're too late," Rita called. "We already been to the swings."

Katie rose, dripping water. "Who cares?" she said. "*I* have been *thinking!*"

And she sloshed off toward the bridge, toward Sue, not paying a bit of attention to the astonished look on Rita's face.

The Sign of the Black Hand

School had started and Katie liked it so well she didn't mind not going to school in New York. Especially she liked her fifth-grade teacher, Miss Howell. Miss Howell was gray and rather old-fashioned, with a sweet, motherly face. She believed in memory work to train the children's minds, and every week she had the class learn a poem—homey old poems like "The Village Blacksmith." "Under a spreading chestnut tree the village smithy stands," Katie and the others would chant on Fridays. Also there were spelling bees, with the teams lined up opposite each other, backs to the blackboards. Katie's heart would pound with the excitement of the spelldowns.

She'd made friends with several girls in the room, but Sue was still her bosom friend, closer than ever since their fight. Katie guessed she was pretty lucky, come to think of it, that Sue didn't already have a best friend. Of course, everyone at school liked Sue, but none of the girls lived nearby.

And Sue didn't spend as much time on that boy as Katie had feared. Mostly it was just a matter of Sue and Bob choosing each other for spelling teams and passing silly notes sometimes.

Katie and Sue were going to give a Halloween party and invite all the girls in their room. They'd have it at Katie's house because it was so spooky.

"It's perfect for Halloween!" Katie John had exclaimed. "We can lead the girls down the dark passage under the back porch and play tricks with the speaking tubes in the walls."

Even though it was only early October, Katie and Sue had all their plans made for the party and their costumes. Katie was to be a gypsy and tell fortunes under the green hanging chandelier in her bedroom. Sue had a pretty shepherdess costume. But, with the plans settled, the time until Halloween stretched long and empty.

Then one Friday night Katie saw something in the newspaper that gave her an idea. And the society of the Sign of the Black Hand was born.

Katie could hardly wait to get down to Sue's house Saturday morning to tell her. Just as she dashed out of the house, though, Mother caught her and made her come back to do her Saturday morning dusting. Katie hated that job—all those crooks and curves on the chair and table legs, all those little vases and knickknacks of Aunt Emily's that had to be picked up so she could dust the mantel and the whatnot.

At last Katie ran down to Sue's house. In the kitchen she found Sue and her big sister, Janet, arguing furiously.

"I won't!" Sue was almost crying.

"Oh, yes, you will, young lady!" Janet snapped. "Mother said!"

Janet was in her pajamas, and the table was still covered with breakfast dishes.

"You never do the dishes any more," Sue cried angrily. "Look at all that messy egg. It'll take all morning to get it off. I won't!"

"Then they'll just sit there," Janet said, gathering up a bottle of shampoo and a hairbrush. "Mother said I didn't have to because I've got to wash my hair for the dance."

"Excuses, always the big excuses," Sue shouted after her sister.

"You're such a child. You just don't understand!" Janet called back as she ran upstairs.

The bathroom door slammed. Sue slumped down in a chair.

"She thinks she's so important, so great and wonderful," Sue said bitterly. "She used to be a pretty good sister, but now that she's in high school and has dates she's just awful. You're lucky you don't have any sisters, Katie."

"I guess so." Katie looked up at the ceiling as the sounds of shower water began. "But look, Sue, I'll help you and we'll get done fast. Because I've got a perfectly marvelous idea."

Katie wouldn't tell about it yet, though. She said they had to go to the barn behind her house first. The egg dishes didn't take all morning, after all, and the girls slipped out without seeing Janet again.

The day was sunny and crisp with autumn, but the inside of the old brick barn was dark and chilly. The girls peered into the dusty storage rooms and saw a jumble of old furniture and tools and rakes and rat traps and a big chair made of buffalo horns and trunks and barrels —and all of it tumbled every which way.

"It looks as if people just opened the door and threw things in," Katie said.

She pulled the buffalo-horn chair loose from the clutter and sat down in it.

"Now then," she said, "I'll tell. We're going to form a secret mysterious club! This can be our meeting place. Just you and I will belong, and we'll call it the Sign of the Black Hand—okay?" she remembered to ask, because she'd vowed not to be so bossy with Sue.

"Wonderful," Sue said cautiously, "but what—?"

"Oh Sue, it's the most exciting thing! You see, it's real! There really is a secret society called the Black Hand! I read about it in the paper last night."

Katie was a little vague about details, but it seemed that a lot of the gangsters all over the United States belonged to this secret club and did all sorts of mysterious things and always left a black handprint where they'd been.

Or maybe they weren't gangsters, but strange dark men. Anyway, this black handprint kept popping up around the country where jewels had been stolen or money had been left in the night on some poor widow's table.

"It sounds scary," Sue said. "What if these men found out about us?"

"Oh, they wouldn't," Katie assured her. "They're just in big cities."

"But we're not going to steal things?" Sue asked in alarm.

"No, silly. We'll do mysterious *good* deeds."

"Like what?"

"Well, like we'll teach Janet a good lesson. We'll teach her not to be so mean to you."

First, Katie said, they had to form their club properly. They went to Katie's house and got a needle, some white paper, scissors, and two black crayons. Back in the barn, they used the needle to prick the palms of their hands until a point of blood showed. They clasped hands and solemnly said the vow they'd made up.

"I do promise always to be loyal to members of the Black Hand and never to tell anyone about the secret good deeds we do."

"There now," Katie said. "We're blood sisters under the Sign of the Black Hand. And whenever we do something we'll leave a black handprint."

She and Sue outlined their hands on the white paper, cut out the hand shapes, colored them black with the crayons, and pinned the hands to their blouses.

"Now, go get Janet," Katie said.

Sue hesitated. "I don't think she'll come."

"Tell her we'll show her a tremendous surprise!"

While Sue was gone, Katie made another black handprint and fastened it to the barn door. Then she rummaged around in the barn until she found an old black velvet piano scarf. She sat down in the buffalo-horn chair, threw the black scarf over her head, and waited. Pretty soon she heard Janet and Sue coming and she sat up straight.

"What is all this kid stuff, anyway?" Janet said, coming in the door.

Katie peeked through the fringe of the scarf and saw that Janet had her hair done up. Janet looked as if she was ready to laugh.

"Janet Halsey, thou miserable creature," Katie said in a loud, booming voice, "stand silent before the awful court of the Sign of the Black Hand!"

"You crazy kids," Janet giggled.

Katie ignored her. "Janet Halsey, on num—number—many times you have made your poor little sister wash the dishes when it was your turn."

Janet glared at Sue, who looked as though she wished she'd never gotten into this.

"The court of the Black Hand orders you to wash the dishes more often," Katie went on solemnly. "Promise?"

"No!" Janet was indignant. "I do more housework than she does already."

"Then the Sign of the Black Hand sentences you to—" Katie paused to think of something dreadful.

"You can't make me do anything," Janet said. She gave a nasty laugh. "If you knew how silly you look under that ragged scarf, Katie Tucker!"

Katie forgot to make her voice slow and booming. "All right for you, Janet Halsey. From now on the Black Hand will—will haunt you!" She had an inspiration. "We'll tell you the honest-to-goodness truth about all your worse faults!"

Janet stopped, disconcerted. Then she gave that laugh again. "So what. I already know them. Go play, children!" And she left.

Katie John tore off the black scarf and threw it on the floor. "Oh, she makes me mad!"

"See what I mean about big sisters?" Sue said. "The worst is, we can't do anything to her."

"Oh yes, we can. We'll fix Miss Janet Halsey, all right," Katie said grimly. "We'll do just what I said."

The two girls put their heads together over the faults of Janet Halsey, and her younger sister knew them right well. Plotting and giggling, the awful members of the Black Hand laid their plans.

They proceeded to the home of the Black Hand Chief and placed a telephone call. In preparation, the Chief placed a marble in her mouth and covered the telephone mouthpiece with a handkerchief.

"May I speak to Janet?" the muffled voice of the Chief asked.

"This is she. Who—"

"If you can answer this question correctly, you will win a fabulous prize. Ready?"

"Yes . . ."

"Why don't you clean out the hair from the wash-bowl when you wash your hair?"

"Wha—oh! Get off this phone, Katie John Tucker!"

"Sorry, you have lost the prize. This is the free advice service of the Black Hand Society. Good-byeee!"

The conspirators then printed on a piece of paper: "You have a pretty face, but your nose is a shade too long." A black hand was drawn under the words. The society members stole into the Halsey house and placed the note in Janet's library book.

Seeing Janet in the kitchen putting cooky sheets into the oven, they advised her, "You make wonderful peanut-butter cookies, Janet. Too bad that's all you can cook."

The members of the Black Hand then decided to let matters rest for a while, giving Janet a chance to worry about when they'd strike next.

When Sue came after Katie that afternoon she reported that Janet had gone to her room to read and come right back out again. She hadn't said a word all through lunch. Now Janet was about to go down to the drugstore to meet some friends for a Coke.

"Good. We'll go too," said Katie.

She and Sue pinned their black hands to their blouses.

"Are we going to say things in front of her friends?" Sue worried. "I mean, that wouldn't be very nice."

"Is Janet nice to you?" Katie demanded.

"No-o, not lately. All right, but let's not be too mean."

"Just mean enough," Katie promised.

They waited outside the Halsey house until Janet came out, and walked down the sidewalk a few steps behind her.

Janet turned around. "You brats quit tagging me."

"Why, we're just walking down the street," Katie John said sweetly.

The procession went on. Janet pretended they weren't there.

At the drugstore she met Carolyn and another girl friend. With much chatter and commotion they swept through the store, back to the booths. James's Drugstore was the teen-age hangout, but Katie and Sue slipped into the booth behind Janet.

They heard Janet tell her friends, "Don't pay any attention to anything those children say. That Katie Tucker is an awful influence on Sue."

Katie and Sue ordered root-beer floats.

"We'll have to start collecting club dues to pay for business expenses like these," Katie whispered.

Raising her voice, she said, "The Society of the Black Hand could give your sister a lot of good advice if she'd just take it." Leaning forward, she called, "For instance, Janet, your telephone voice."

Janet talked loudly about the dance that night.

"No, you should listen, Janet. You have a very pleasant telephone voice," Katie continued. "The only trouble is when you talk to boys. Then you get a sort of little-girl whine. I wonder if it's as effective as you think."

Carolyn and the other girl giggled, and Janet slowly turned a deep pink. However, she spoke with control and dignity.

"I do not care to discuss my voice with you, Miss Tucker. But for your information, I do all right for dates."

Her date for the football dance tonight was the star football quarterback, and her friends knew it. They nodded and sympathized with Janet about snotty little sisters and their pals.

"Well," Katie pitched her voice to pierce, "it's a shame your mother can't do something about Janet. Like making her mend things more often. To see Janet all dressed up, you'd never know that, underneath, all her underclothes are held together with safety pins. She's got so many pins on her slip straps and things, it's a wonder she doesn't rattle when she walks."

During this speech conversation had come to a halt

in the next booth. Now Janet's friends let out screams of laughter.

"I'm sorry, Janet," Carolyn gasped, "but really . . . !"

Janet half-rose from her seat and spit out, "If you don't go home right now—I'll—I'll—"

Katie and Sue scrambled out of their booth. "Why, Janet, we're just leaving," Katie smiled. "It's just too bad you won't take the advice of the Black Hand." She unpinned the black paper hand from her blouse and tossed it down by Janet's Coke. "Because we have such a lot of it."

"Yes," Sue said primly, smoothing her skirts.

After they'd marched out of the drugstore, though, Sue sighed. "I don't think it did a bit of good, Katie. Now she's so mad she'll just treat me worse."

"Wait and see if she does the dishes tonight," Katie advised.

They left Janet alone for the rest of the day. After supper Katie went down to Sue's house to find out if the Black Hand had reformed Janet. However, she waited on the porch for Sue. The night air was soft with Indian summer, and there was a gorgeous yellow harvest moon. Besides, Mrs. Halsey just might be mad, if Janet had told her. Maybe they had been too rough on Janet—at least the part at the drugstore.

Sue shook her head mournfully when she came out. "I did them again. Mother told me to because Janet has to get ready for the dance. And Janet won't even speak to me."

Katie's wavering resolution was immediately strengthened. "Then she hasn't had enough. Come on."

"No, Katie. I don't want to do any more."

"Fellow member of the Black Hand," Katie said, "we are in this together, and we mustn't quit now. We mustn't fail on our very first good deed."

Sue sighed, but followed Katie around the house to the ground-floor window of the bedroom she and her sister shared. The girls looked in and saw Janet sitting at her dressing table in her slip. There were no pins on the straps.

And Janet looked so different, somehow. Katie forgot why she was there as she watched the older girl perform the ritual of beauty, outlining her lips, dabbing perfume on her wrists. Janet's shoulders gleamed smooth and round, and her face was alive with the excitement of the evening. Around her the room was full of Janet's preparations: there was her frothy party dress, there were her new spiky shoes, there was her beaded evening purse on the bed. In the soft pink light of the bed lamp, the room glowed like a jewel case. And Janet was the jewel.

Why, she's a young lady, Katie realized. Almost a woman. Will it be like this for me someday? Will I sit before a mirror someday with the room soft and pink around me? Will I be lovely? The thoughts floated dreamily.

Janet was getting into her dress now, and Mrs. Halsey came in to help her.

Janet caught sight of the girls at the window and cried, "Mother, make those kids go away!"

She didn't seem to have told her mother what Katie and Sue had been doing. Maybe because she was in such a tizzy about the dance. Sue had said earlier that she believed Janet was secretly scared to be going with the football player, he was such a school hero.

"Run along, girls," Mrs. Halsey murmured, hooking the back of Janet's dress.

Katie sighed without knowing it. Out here in the dark, looking into the lighted room, it was like watching a play, seeing the first steps to being a woman. Slowly she stepped back and watched from the shadows. Sue joggled her elbow to remind her of their purpose, but Katie shook her head, eyes fixed on the girl inside.

Now Janet was poking at her hair nervously. It was pulled up, with an elaborate arrangement of curls waterfalling down the back.

"Oh, Mother!" she wailed. "It won't go right! It looks terrible!"

"No! It's beautiful! You look beautiful!" The protest burst from Katie John.

Janet whirled, her face angry, as if she'd been expecting more "advice" from Katie. Then, as she realized what Katie had said, her face softened in surprise. She didn't speak, however, but turned back to the finishing touches of her dressing.

A car had driven up. Janet's date was at the front door. Katie moved around to the front yard, and Sue followed, looking at Katie in amazement.

Janet came out the door, laughing with the boy. She saw Katie standing at the edge of the walk.

"Katie, that was sweet of you." She smiled. Lightly she touched Katie's arm. "Thanks. Thanks for the honest-to-goodness truth!"

She swept on out to the car. The door slammed, and the car roared away.

Katie turned and saw Sue still staring at her.

"Well, it was the truth," she muttered. "You know," she added thoughtfully, "I'll bet Janet does the dishes for you tomorrow."

The Good House

It was November-cold as Katie John walked home from the library. Dusk had sifted down from the gray sky, and the street lights were already lit. The wind, whipping through bare branches, made Katie huddle deep into her coat. She clutched a pile of library books to her chest, smiling at the warm feeling she got from them. She'd picked out such good ones this time. Another one about Jane, a new book of fairy tales, and a book about a girl in Revolutionary War times that looked exciting. She could hardly wait to curl up in the big chair and start reading. Which one, though? They all looked so good. The one about Jane, she decided. The Moffats were so cozy, just right for a cold winter evening.

Katie rounded the corner onto her block, and the wind pushed straight at her now. At the end of the block, at the top of the hill, she could see her house, one light shining yellow out of an upstairs window. The tree branches around the house flung about in the wind, but the house itself rose square and solid above them.

It's like a ship, riding out a storm, Katie thought. No, more like a great lighthouse, standing steady as a rock with all the storm swirling around it. And the light is a beacon for me.

In a spurt against the wind, Katie ran up the hill and into the house. She pushed the door shut and stopped in the hall. How quiet the house was, after the noise of the wind outside. So still and warm. Yet alive with a murmur of little sounds. Katie stood there, holding her books, soaking in the warmth, listening. That soft rumble under her feet was the stoker in the furnace coming on. That distant tap-tap-tap was her father working at his typewriter upstairs . . . tap-tap-tap, ping, went the bell faintly. A rattle of a pan lid said Mother was back in the kitchen. Katie sniffed. Oh good! Hamburgers and onions, with mashed potatoes and gravy, her favorite supper.

Now in the stillness she heard the tock-tock of the old marble clock in the parlor. It's like the sound of the house, ticking away at its business, she thought. She turned to look in at the clock on the mantelpiece. Why, it had been ticking there for almost a hundred years, ever since Great-Grandpa brought it home in the wheelbarrow.

Lovingly, Katie looked at all the signs of the Clark family, gleaming in soft lamplight or shadowy in corners —the polished dark woods, the vases and china collected over the years, Great-Grandfather's paintings on the walls, Great-Aunt Emily's crocheted doilies on Katie's reading chair. Her fingers smoothed the yellow wood of the door-frame. The good house that Great-Grandfather built. The good home.

Suddenly Katie John knew why Aunt Emily had never left this house, never gone away for new adventure when it was clear that she wouldn't marry.

Because this was home.

As simple as that. Because this was where she belonged.

The next thought came as surely as summer follows spring: *This is where I belong, too.*

Katie felt such a spreading in her chest that she wanted to stretch out her arms. Oh, she loved this house! She loved Barton's Bluff. She even loved Miss Crackenberry and that crazy Prince. Because they were all a part of living here.

She dropped her books on the big chair and tossed her coat at the hall hatrack as Dad came clattering down the stairs.

"Oh, Dad!" She ran to him. The words for all that she wanted to say choked in her throat. "Dad, come quick!"

She pulled him back to the kitchen. She had to say it to both of them.

"Dad, Mother, the house—let's stay! Let's not sell the house. Let's just stay here. Let's live here always!"

"Oh now, Katie," Dad began, laughing.

But Mother looked at her with a sad little smile. "I know, Katie. I know. If only we could—"

Dad wasn't laughing now. "I'd like to stay, too. It's a good house, and we're happy here. I don't have to live in New York to write. But—"

The facts hadn't changed. They still needed the sale money from the house to live on until he started earning money from his books.

Dad rubbed his face. "There's something else. This is a bad time to tell you. But we'll just have to face it."

Someone wanted to buy the house. It was the fat man who had wanted to turn it into a rooming house.

Katie's mind spun back to the day he'd come, the day she had learned so much about Aunt Emily. He had spit on the fire screen. He wanted to squeeze in lots of roomers. Make some money from the house before it fell apart, he said.

"He made a pretty good offer," Dad was saying. "Came near our asking price. I'm afraid we'll have to—"

"No!" Katie cried. "No no no!"

He wouldn't take care of the house. He said he didn't want to spend money on repairs. And an old house needed lots of care. Dad had said the house needed a new roof. With all those people, the place would get rattletrap and dirty, start to fall apart. She'd seen some of the old homes that were now rooming houses, boardinghouses. Crumbling steps, broken windows, paint cracked, washing flapping on the porches. No!

Katie argued. She begged. At last she cried. She

stopped when she saw that Mother and Dad looked almost ready to cry, too.

All through the miserable supper that no one ate, Katie's thoughts wound drearily. So they'd leave the house. Go live in some dinky little New York apartment. Oh, a person could be happy anywhere. Sure. But this was home. And then to think of that man spitting on the house, the hordes of people moving in and out and none of them loving it, and it crumbling away.

The hamburger tasted like soggy cardboard in her mouth, and she could hardly swallow it. Money. Hateful, horrible stuff. Where could they get some money, so they could stay?

If only she and Sue could have found a sack of gold hidden away somewhere in the house when they were looking for secret places. Or if Great-Aunt Emily had left some money. But all she'd left was the house. And old houses were so big and expensive to keep up, they weren't good for anything any more but to rent out rooms.

Oh, if only the fat man even loved the house, Katie thought in despair. Then at least he might take care of it.

Wait. What was that? Rent out rooms but take care of the house. Ye-es-s, yes! Why couldn't they do it instead of that man?

Katie started to blurt it out. Then she stopped. Dad might say, "No, Katie," and not really understand the idea. Better to think it all out and then tell them.

After supper Katie hurried right off to bed, leaving her

parents sighing because they thought she was so unhappy. But she had to be alone, now, and in bed was the best place for thinking things through. Now she must be careful. She couldn't go whizzing at this idea in her usual way. This was serious business. Their last chance. She had to get it just right, so it would make sense to grownups.

As Katie threw off her clothes, though, she felt a doubt. Was it worth it? Would it be the same, would the house still be home with renters in it? She didn't want to share her home with a lot of other people.

It's better than nothing, she told herself firmly. It will still be our house.

She scrambled under the covers and began to figure. Now it was clear they'd have to rent out most of the house, if they were to make enough money to live on. They must live on just the first floor. She'd have to give her pretty bedroom to her folks, she realized with a twinge of regret. She could sleep in the little room off the kitchen.

Then they could rent all the rooms on the second and third floors. And the basement, too. Yes, the little servants' apartment, where the dumb-waiter ended up, would be nice for someone. And oh, what a lucky thing that Aunt Emily had put in so many bathrooms!

But would anyone want to rent rooms in an old house? They should get nice people who would take care of their rooms. What could be special about the rooms?

Why, the fireplaces! Every room had a fireplace. So far Dad had lit the little fireplace in the kitchen, and Katie loved dressing before the open brick hearth on cold mornings.

Everyone loves a fireplace, she reasoned, and here they could have one of their own even in a rented room. Some of the fireplaces were really beautiful, too, with carving around the edges and lacy iron or painted fire screens. Yes, the fireplaces could be the drawing card.

Katie John was getting sleepy now; her plans were fuzzy at the edges. Tomorrow she'd tell Mother and Dad about it . . . so good to know things were working out. So good that the house had bathrooms and fireplaces and big rooms for renters. The house would save itself, after all . . . or maybe it was Great-Grandfather who was saving it, because of the way he'd built the house, she thought drowsily. And Aunt Emily. All the Clarks had put so much into the house. Because they loved it.

And what had she herself put into the house? The thought woke her up a little. Nothing, really. Well, she was probably the only person outside of the builder who knew what the inside of the dumb-waiter walls looked like. But that wasn't doing anything. She would, she promised herself. Someday she'd do something for the old house.

The next morning Katie decided not to tell her folks yet. It was a good plan. But grownups had such a habit of saying "No, Katie" to good plans. Better if they could actually see it working out. Upon waking up, it had been quite plain what she must do: find a renter.

What's more, she knew just the person. Her teacher, Miss Howell. Not long ago Miss Howell had been saying that soon she and her sister must move into town from their farm for the winter. They lived out on a hill above the river in their old homeplace. Now that she understood so much more, Katie guessed they must love their house as she did hers. But it was too cold and icy for two old ladies to live out there alone in the winter. So, as Miss Howell had been telling her when she was helping after school the other day, every winter they moved into an apartment in town. And they hadn't found one yet.

As Katie walked to school she grew more and more excited as she figured how a little kitchen could be put in one of the rooms upstairs, so that Miss Howell could have a big two-room-and-bath apartment. She was so wrapped up in plans that she forgot to stop for Sue. Later at school she explained to Sue that she had something very big brewing, and she'd tell her tonight if it worked out.

Katie almost burst before recess time. When the bell rang she stayed in the room and told Miss Howell all about it. About loving the house and wanting to stay and renting out rooms. Then she was afraid it sounded as though she were begging. So as not to put Miss Howell on the spot, she said hastily:

"Of course, you mustn't do it just to help us out. You

shouldn't rent the apartment unless you really like it."
And couldn't help adding honestly, "But I hope you do."

Miss Howell, who had listened carefully, smiled now.
"I understand, Katie John. Of course I want to help you.
But I promise you I won't rent it unless it will suit Julia
and me. After all, we're the ones who will have to live
there all winter."

Miss Howell pointed out that it would also depend on
how much the rent would be. She thought that Katie
should talk it over with her parents first. But Katie had
her plans fixed.

"Please, just look at the rooms first," she said. "Then
if you're already interested, Mother and Dad will think
about it more seriously."

So Miss Howell said that she'd come home with Katie
after school. Katie could hardly keep her mind on school-
work for the rest of the day. She made all the circles in
penmanship slant the wrong way because she was thinking
about the one last important detail. How would she work
out that part? Maybe she shouldn't—it might make
Mother and Dad mad. . . . But it would make everything so perfect. Katie pushed at her bangs. She just had
to do it. If only her folks would be out, just once, when
she got home from school.

As it happened, Miss Howell had to stay after school
for a parent conference. She said she'd drive down to
Katie's house afterward. But that was fine. It would give
Katie plenty of time to finish that last detail.

"Got to hurry," she told Sue after school. "I'll run on ahead and see you later. Tell you all about it then."

Sue looked disappointed but nodded patiently. Oh, what a joy it was to have a good friend like Sue! Another reason for staying in Barton's Bluff. Let Miss Howell like the rooms, Katie prayed, as she ran.

Mother and Dad were just coming out the front door when Katie got home. They were going down to Mr. Follensbee's real estate office to talk over plans for selling the house to the fat man.

"You're not going to sign anything already?" Katie cried.

Dad shrugged unhappily. "Honey, you know it's got to be done. But no, we won't be signing anything today. We'll be right back."

"Be sure you don't," Katie said. "We may not have to sell the house yet!"

She heard Mother say as they went down the walk, "Poor child. She's hoping for a miracle." And Katie giggled, almost about to burst with excitement. Little did they know!

She ran down to the basement for the things she needed and took them upstairs. When she had that all ready, she set about making the apartment look as handsome as possible, dusting, opening curtains, taking dust covers off the furniture. She'd chosen two big rooms with a connecting bathroom. The front room overlooked the river, and the back room could be partitioned into a bedroom and kitchen, she'd decided. It already had a wash-bowl that could be used for washing dishes.

The doorbell rang. It must be Miss Howell. Katie did the last important thing. Then she raced down the stairs and brought her teacher in.

"Mother and Dad went to the real estate office, but they'll be right back," Katie told her. "I'll show you the apartment."

Katie's hands were suddenly cold and she clasped them in front of her as she led Miss Howell up the stairs. Miss Howell's warm voice was saying nice things about how beautiful the house was, but now Katie couldn't answer. The important thing was, what would she think of the apartment?

Along the hall . . . open the door . . . Katie gasped.

Smoke! Black smoke billowed in the room and poured out the doorway.

"The house is on fire!" Katie screamed. "Quick! Water!"

She ran to get water from the bathroom somehow. And then she saw that the room wasn't on fire, after all. The wretched black smoke was pouring from the fire-place—the beautiful fireplace, where she'd worked so hard laying wood. That had been the important thing that was to make it all perfect. She wanted Miss Howell to be greeted by a homey blaze when she looked into the room. Just before she'd run downstairs she'd lit the fire.

And now look! Smoke filled the room, and more was coming out all the time. The wood was burning, but the smoke wasn't going up the chimney.

"We must put out the fire quickly!" Miss Howell scooped up the empty coal bucket from the hearth and ran to the bathroom for water.

Katie ran after her, sobbing and getting in the way.

"No, you open the windows," Miss Howell said, hurrying back to the fireplace.

Fortunately, the fire hadn't gotten well started yet, and the blaze died under the water.

"Oh, look at the room!" Katie wailed. "It'll be black with smoke!"

She beat at the smoke, trying to push it out the window before it settled on the walls and the white curtains. The fire reduced to wet black ashes, Miss Howell rushed to help Katie, fanning the smoke with a sheaf of school papers.

"What in the world!"

Katie turned and saw her horrified parents coming into the room.

"It's all my fault!" she cried in despair. "I wanted to make a nice fire, but the smoke didn't go up the chimney."

"Because the chimney is capped! All of them are except the one for the kitchen." Dad's face was angry. "Young lady, I—"

"Oh, wouldn't you know!" Katie sobbed. "Everything I do goes wrong!"

"Let's get the smoke out of here first," Mother suggested.

She and Dad joined Miss Howell in fanning smoke out the windows while Katie poured out the whole story.

"I knew I shouldn't have lit that fire," she ended miserably, "but it seemed like such a wonderful idea. And now look."

She stared at the soupy mass of ashes in the fireplace.

"Well," Dad said slowly, "of course you shouldn't have lit the fire without a grownup around—you do get carried away with your ideas, Katie. But basically you had a pretty good plan, at that."

In fact, he'd been thinking about renting out apartments, too, he said. He'd figured that from the rents they could pay for the upkeep of the big house and have a little left over.

"We can't do it, though, Katie," he added quickly. "I soon realized that running an apartment house would throw entirely too much work on your mother. And we couldn't afford to hire help."

Then Mother made a confession. She too had been thinking about renting, had even checked on rental regulations. But, according to fire laws, they couldn't have women and children on the third floor, only men. So that meant she'd have to do all the weekly cleaning and laundry for those rooms, plus all the general work of taking care of an apartment house.

"I just don't see how I could do it all alone," she sighed, "and I won't have you leave your writing to do it," she told her husband.

He shook his head sadly. "I could do the repair work and take care of the furnace. But it would still leave too great a burden on you. We'll just have to forget it."

Katie had been looking from one parent to another. Well, for goodness' sakes! So she had been on the right track, with her idea about renting. For once she'd thought something through almost like a grownup would! Her chest stopped feeling so tight.

But still, it didn't do any good. They had to leave, just the same. Renting rooms meant too much work for Mother. Katie sighed. It was just too bad that she wasn't big enough to help.

And then Katie began to get all hot inside, the way she always did when she was about to have a wonderful idea. Just how big did she have to be to help? How big, to sweep down the stairs that renters would dirty, to make beds, hang sheets on the line, dust furniture, vacuum floors? She could do those things.

But all that work! Katie shuddered. I'm just a little girl. I hate housework. It would take so much time.

"I could do it," she heard herself saying. "I could help. I could work after school and on Saturdays."

Mother smiled but shook her head. "It's really sweet of you, Katie. But you're just a little girl. I have to stand over you even to get you to dust your room."

"I know! I know!" Katie cried desperately. "But I can change! Now I want to work. If only we can stay here!"

She had to make them understand. To make them know how much she wanted to stay, enough to do all that work. The words tumbled out until Mother interrupted.

"Why, you've really made up your mind, haven't you!" She laughed. "And I know you, Katie John. When you set your mind on something, you stick to it. I do believe I can depend on you!" She turned to Dad. "Dear, let's try it!"

Dad looked from Mother to Katie John. He threw up his hands and laughed. "It's all right with me. You women will be doing all the work!"

All the tensely held breath went out of Katie. "Oh, Daddy!" She flung herself at him.

While he hugged her he said that after he started earning money from his book they could hire a cleaning woman. And Mother said they'd get things organized so Katie wouldn't have to work all the time. But Katie hardly heard. All she could think was: We're staying! We're staying!

Miss Howell had been wandering around the rooms, and now she came back to the Tuckers.

"May I have the honor of being your first renter?" she asked with a twinkle in her smile.

Despite the smoky fireplace, she said—and Dad hastily said he'd uncap the chimneys—she liked the rooms and was sure her sister would, too.

That made things perfect, but all Katie could do was reach out and squeeze her teacher's hand. Dad and Mother and Miss Howell went off to the second room to discuss how they could partition it and put in a stove and refrigerator. Katie walked out into the hallway.

And so they would stay. The old Clark house would go on, with the Tucker family in it. And the renters, too. Wonder who they'd be? Why, it could be fun, Katie realized with a little prick of excitement, having all sorts of people—nice ones and maybe ornery ones—coming to live here. And she and Mother would take care of them.

A warm, satisfied feeling spread through Katie, clear down to her stomach, because everything had worked out so well. Even the answer to that question that had been bothering her last night: What could she do for the old house to match the loving care of Great-Grandfather and Great-Aunt Emily? Her work. All that pesky housework that would help them keep the house.

Katie John looked up the stairwell to the top of the house, then down to the hall below. She started down the stairs, sliding her fingers along the banister.

"Hello, home," she said softly.

HARPER TROPHY BOOKS

you will enjoy reading

HARPER & ROW, PUBLISHERS, INC.
10 East 53rd Street, New York, New York 10022